Working-Class Heroes

Working-Class Heroes

*Protecting Home, Community, and Nation
in a Chicago Neighborhood*

MARIA KEFALAS

UNIVERSITY OF CALIFORNIA PRESS

Berkeley   Los Angeles   London

University of California Press
Berkeley and Los Angeles, California

University of California Press, Ltd.
London, England

Library of Congress Cataloging-in-Publication Data

Kefalas, Maria.
    Working-class heroes : protecting home, community, and
nation in a Chicago neighborhood / Maria Kefalas.
        p.   cm.
    Includes bibliographical references and index.
    ISBN 978-0-520-23543-4 (paper : alk. paper)

    1. Chicago (Ill.)—Social conditions.   2. Working class—
Illinois—Chicago.   3. Sociology, Urban—Illinois—Chicago.
4. Social values—Illinois—Chicago.   5. Chicago (Ill.)—Race
relations.   6. Beltway (Chicago, Ill.)   I. Title.
HN80.C5 K43   2003
306.09773'11—dc21   2002005541

Manufactured in the United States of America

12   11   10
10   9   8   7   6   5   4

The paper used in this publication is both acid-free and totally
chlorine-free (TCF). It meets the minimum requirements of
ANSI/NISO Z39.48–1992 (R 1997) (*Permanence of Paper*).

This book is dedicated to my parents, John and Alice Kefalas, who instilled within me a curiosity about "what makes people tick," and to the courageous men and women of Beltway who shared their stories and opinions with me.

CONTENTS

MAPS AND TABLES

MAPS

TABLES

ACKNOWLEDGMENTS

When my lovely daughter was born in March 2000, I joked to my friends that Camille would replace my first baby, this book. I am afraid there is more than a little truth in the notion that this work has been like a child I have nurtured since my earliest days of graduate school in 1993. I am very protective of the people I describe in this book, and I am terrified about not living up to the responsibility of getting the story right. Once a book is written though, how readers interpret the final product is beyond the author's control. It is impossible to please everyone. However, it is my greatest wish that this work will provide an accurate and fair accounting of what it means to live in places such as Beltway.

All books born from dissertations exist because of the help, guidance, support, insight, and intellect of others. Even though writing is a lonely enterprise, generating ideas and analysis is actually quite dynamic and very much a group process. I will be the first to admit that the best parts of this book exist because of the work of others.

First, I must thank the Principal Investigators of the Comparative Neighborhood Study, William J. Wilson and Richard Taub, who made it possible for me to conduct research in Beltway. I am also grateful to my talented colleagues on the project: Erin Augis, Patrick Carr, Chenoa Flippen, Jennifer Johnson, Reuben May, Jeffrey Morenoff, Jennifer Pashup,

Mary Patillo, and Jolyon Wurr, who helped me formulate many of the central ideas for the book in our challenging project meetings. Professor Wilson also served on my dissertation committee and over the past eight years has pushed and prodded me to use passion and clarity when I express my ideas. Robert Sampson's exceptional courses on urban and community studies enlightened and educated me about the grand tradition of the Chicago School. In 1996, John Laub graciously agreed to sit on my committee one night over dinner in Boston. I will always be grateful for his willingness to take on this task, and my work has benefited immensely from his penetrating critiques and "insider" status as a born and bred Chicagoan. Professor Gerald Suttles, upon his retirement from the University of Chicago, remarked that all graduate students have one good idea; I will always be indebted to him for helping me give this idea life. Kathy Edin, whom I first met while a wet-behind-ears graduate student, took me under her wing, gave me a job, and demanded (in her inimitably Midwestern manner) that I be rigorous about my methods and honor the process of ethnography. As a postdoctoral researcher at the University of Pennsylvania, I also had the great fortune of meeting Michèle Lamont. Professor Lamont's keen interest in my work on working- and lower-middle-class whites and her firm belief in the timeliness of Beltway's story encouraged me during that crucial final period of revisions.

I cannot express how much I owe my mentor and friend Wendy Griswold, who dedicated dozens of hours to this project. Even when she was on sabbatical in Italy, she managed to send me detailed comments on more drafts of this manuscript then either of us cares to remember. She was one of the first people to be convinced that the people of Beltway had a great story to tell. Professor Griswold has been a firm taskmaster and my loudest cheerleader, and there is no question that this book would not have existed without her. For five years she has encouraged me to finish with the gentle reminder that she has saved a special place for it on her bookshelf. I should also thank Wendy's daughter Olivia, who allowed me to intrude on their Wednesday afternoons together at the Medici.

Numerous other people have read the manuscript over the years, and their comments and insights have become woven into the final product. Special thanks to Gary Alan Fine, Andrew Abbott, Robert Bursik Jr., Herbert Gans, Richard Taub, Martin Riesenbrodt, Claudio Lomnitz, Dawne Moon, Joseph Bigott, Jennifer Pashup, Patrick Carr, Marcellus Andrews, Mark Jacobs, Richard Warren, Albert Hunter, Philip Kasinitz, Dalton Conley, and past and present participants of the Culture and Society Workshop. Jeffrey Morenoff also provided some marvelous maps of Chicago at a moment's notice. Carmen Croce, Debra Leone, Carol McLaughlin, and Thomas Mallone, all of St. Joseph's University Press, created additional maps and tables and prepared the artwork.

Aspects of this work were presented at a variety of colloquia and institutions including SUNY-Albany, Barnard College, the University of Pennsylvania, Princeton University, the University of Chicago, and American Sociological Association meetings. Financial support for the project came from the MacArthur Foundation, Wellesley College, the University of Chicago, and St. Joseph's University.

My wonderful editor at the University of California Press, Naomi Schneider, has graciously worked around my schedule as new professor and a new mother to help me complete this book. I marvel at her ability to read 50 pages of a manuscript and have a page and a half of comments back to me in 24 hours (with just the right mix of constructive criticism and encouragement).

Even though I am obligated to protect the identities of the people in this book I must thank by name Linda, Judy, Pastor Judy, Rich and Marie, Mary, A.S., the members of the Civic League, and friends from the Bunco Squad. Special thanks to Beltway's aldermen (past and present) and Congressman William Lipinski.

My family has always provided support (financial, emotional, and psychic) through the long apprenticeship required of scholars. To my mother, I am grateful for your determination and toughness. To my father, thank you for your advice and unwavering pride. My sisters Nicole

Orcutt and Catherine Schidelbauer and my brother Robert Kefalas have kept me grounded while pushing me because they never doubted my ability to complete any task set before me. Their excitement about "Aunt Ria's book" has inspired me over the years.

My daughter Camille was born just as I had finished the first draft. She has forced me to be brutally efficient with my time and always forgives me for being distracted by the dog-eared pile of papers I carry around with me in an overstuffed briefcase. Camille Josephine, you are a dear, sweet creature, and I am not sure what I did to deserve you.

Finally, there is no way to express my love and appreciation to the graduate student from Ireland who told me about "a great job with Bill Wilson" and helped me see I might have a knack for interviewing and fieldwork. He has been with me from the very beginning and has generously shared his talent. You have never complained once about my messy office, my late night work sessions, or the extra housework you always end up doing. To my dearest Pat, I owe you more than any words can say.

In Search of Working-Class Chicago

Chicago served as one of the first laboratories for early social scientists. For nearly a century, scholars from the University of Chicago have taken to the streets to examine life in urban America. American sociology was born in the city's dilapidated neighborhoods of crowded tenements and cold-water flats. In 1907, Upton Sinclair's literary masterpiece *The Jungle* created a devastating portrait of life in Chicago's South Side slums and awakened Americans to the hardships faced by immigrant laborers and their families.[1] Yet today, almost 100 years later, the working-class descendants of these immigrants who toiled in Chicago's factories, stockyards, and railroads—the white ethnics—have received almost no attention from contemporary scholars. Maybe it is because Americans have largely defined themselves as citizens of a classless, meritocratic society, or maybe it is because a disproportionate percentage of Americans see themselves as middle class. Whatever the reasons, scholars have turned a blind eye to examining the lives of more modestly employed urban ethnic whites.

The peculiar difficulties inherent in defining who exactly comprises the working class exacerbates the challenges of chronicling the lives of this segment of American society. Dated categories of blue- and pink-collar work no longer describe the texture of working-class labor, and as a result, more complex and nuanced thinking is needed.[2] Michèle Lamont, a sociologist whose work considers the cultural boundaries created around class and race, defines "working-class men and women as blue-collar and lower-middle class workers with stable employment and high-school diplomas, but not college degrees, which means that they face severe barriers in access to jobs and other social benefits." Lamont continues, "in a time when the upper middle class is becoming more isolated socially and geographically from other groups, such isolation fosters a social myopia that makes it increasingly difficult for the college-educated, academics, and policy makers to see how distinctive a working-class understanding of the world is."[3]

The few studies of white working-class life that do exist (namely, Lillian Rubin's *Worlds of Pain,* David Halle's *America's Working Man,* William Kornblum's *Blue Collar Community,* Rick Fantasia's *Cultures of Solidarity,* and Jonathan Rieder's *Canarsie*) provide portraits of life in the 1960s and 1970s and tend to focus on race relations or shop floor life. Michèle Lamont's *The Dignity of Working Men* and John Hartigan's *Racial Situations* are the first modern studies of blue-collar Americans to appear in over a decade.

However, as scholarly interest in the urban white working class waned, attention to racialized notions of the inner city and the underclass flourished.[4] By the late 1970s, public and scholarly discourse on urban life focused almost exclusively on the plight of ghetto neighborhoods. Race, poverty, and the inner city have become inextricably linked in the public consciousness, and most Americans assume, albeit incorrectly, that low-income African Americans residing in inner cities make up the overwhelming majority of Americans living in poverty. Few Americans even realize that large numbers of the poor are whites residing in rural areas.[5]

Yet while modern-day studies of working-class whites are few and far between, *historical* accounts of blue-collar urban dwellers abound. Since 1996, historians such as John McGreevey, Gerald Gamm, Wendell Pritchett, and Thomas Sugrue have written about the "urban villages" ethnic whites created during the first part of the twentieth century. Historians' interest in the ethnic enclave story mirrors growing public and academic interest in inner-city ghettoes and the underclass. To such experts, the form of the modern-day ghetto can be directly traced back to the racist interests of working-class whites. According to these scholars, blue-collar white ethnics were more prone than other groups to racial violence because they felt they had the most to lose if integration came to pass. From the vantage point of racist working-class whites, the arrival of blacks violated racial norms of conduct, threatened to spread poverty and crime, and meant the demise of precious local institutions such as the parish. Furthermore, ethnic whites' "peasant" sensibilities concerning the significance of land fueled the white population's all-consuming drive to achieve the goal of home-ownership.[6] From this perspective, the distinctively working-class white desire to own a home, in conjunction with the institutional need of Catholic parishes to maintain strong spatial claims to the community in which a congregation's members lived, set the stage for the racist extremism of white ethnics.

Even though these historical arguments offer important insights into the development of working-class urban whites' racist belief systems, for intellectuals and policymakers it often seems as if ethnic whites have become convenient scapegoats for racism in the same way that the ghetto and its residents are scapegoats for working-class whites' denial and fear. Such accounts of urban history may offer soothing relief for upper-middle-class white guilt over the state of race relations in the postindustrial city, but these versions of history do little to challenge conventional wisdom about race, racism, and racists.

To comprehend the complexities of race, class, and urbanism in the twenty-first century, it is not enough to document the hardships of the oppressed and assign blame. As a society, we must also endeavor to understand how anxiety, anger, hostility, and resentment impede tolerance; indeed, tolerance only comes after every voice of dissent is heard. At the heart of this book is a desire to give a voice to a segment of the population we know very little about beyond the media accounts of bussing and desegregation throughout the 1960s and 1970s.

The inhabitants of Beltway,[7] a working-class neighborhood located on Chicago's Southwest Side, are usually an engaging, straightforward, generous, boisterous, open, patriotic, warm, and trusting lot. At other times, they can be angry, resentful, jealous, insecure, bigoted, ignorant, and downright petty. What many people might find most surprising is that Beltwayites do not explicitly teach their children to hate others because of skin color. They believe in the ideals of justice, liberty, and fair play. More than any other segment of American society, they see purity and truth in the promise of the American Dream.

My purpose in telling the story of one Chicago neighborhood is to show how race relations have evolved since the Civil Rights era, and how complex views of race define residents' distinctive *sense of place*. As ethnographer, interviewer, and scholar, I am the reader's guide into the world Beltway dwellers labor to create. This book should leave the reader with an understanding of how the people I describe make sense of the world.

THE GHETTO AND THE GARDEN

Sociologist Gerald Suttles describes working-class neighborhoods like Chicago's Beltway as defended neighborhoods, in other words, local areas threatened by social or ecological change.[8] In previous ethnographic accounts (notably Jonathan Rieder's impressive study of working- and lower-middle-class Jews and Italians in Canarsie), scholars have painstakingly documented working-class urban whites' terror of neighborhood turnover. On one level, the story of Chicago's Beltway during the 1990s continues where Rieder's story of Brooklyn's Canarsie of the 1970s and 1980s leaves off. Neither place has stood frozen in time. While Rieder chronicles how local activists work to keep out poor blacks, my portrait of neighborhood life in Beltway demonstrates what residents want to defend, and most important, what they would mourn the loss of if the neighborhood ceased to exist. This work explores the ways in which the neighborhood symbolizes everything its working-class residents value—hard work, honesty, patriotism, and respectability—and the fact that the people of Beltway are ready to defend their sense of place at any cost. "Echoing the words of conservative politicians, the people of Beltway view themselves as the protectors of civilization in an imperiled world. This conviction is expressed through the care with which they keep their homes clean, cultivate their gardens, maintain their property, and celebrate the nation. The neighborhood's working- and lower-middle-class residents inscribe their class-bound moral values into their physical surroundings as they fortify moral and symbolic boundaries against the social forces that threaten their way of life."[9]

When I first arrived in Beltway, I planned to document how residents use and interpret race in their everyday lives. Over four years of participating in and observing life in Beltway forced me not so much to alter as to expand my thinking to incorporate what geographers have termed the sense of place—in other words, the meaning people attach to place. What Beltway residents want to defend goes beyond the old notions of racial antagonisms and fears. The people of Beltway seem to share a collective understanding of how their place ought to look and, in a philosophical sense, how its residents ought to be. Neighbors act on this shared sense of place; it inspires them to decorate their front yards for Christmas and imbues them with a sense of outrage at the sight of graffiti. This profound and pervasive sense of place serves as a catalyst for civic activism in response to even the smallest violations of the visual landscape. At the same time, nonwhites—specifically Mexican Americans—are cautiously welcomed to the community as long as they show themselves to be good neighbors who maintain their property and care for their children. Individuals who violate the landscape—and that includes other working-class whites—become the objects of scorn and derision.

Through a powerful sense of place, Beltway residents have created a complex cognitive-emotional geography of home that configures the good life on three levels: that of the household, the community, and the nation. In this study of Beltway, I demonstrate how keeping a fastidious house, standing in a dreary rain-soaked parking lot to commemorate Memorial Day, and generating more effective collective action over graffiti than gang-related violence become explicable and culturally rational when one understands the central myth of *the last garden*. In the pages that follow, I will carry on the Chicago School's tradition of street-level scholarship as I examine life in that garden. I believe that the stories of the men and women of Beltway offer provocative insights into the nature of working-class life in an American city at the dawn of the twenty-first century.

•   •   •

In the 1970s, when African Americans from Chicago's West Side ghetto started migrating to Oak Park, community leaders set up a housing counseling program. Blacks who wanted to move to Oak Park, a comfortable middle-class town known for its fine examples of Frank Lloyd Wright architecture, "were helped to analyze their housing needs and advised to consider other suburbs. The program was a success, in that Oak Park never experienced rapid racial change, as had nearby city neighborhoods. It remained a solidly middle-class place, and its approach to managed integration was praised nationally."[10] Can you imagine what the reaction would be if a similar program were set up in Southwest Side neighborhoods like Beltway? Residents and local activists would be accused of outright racial steering. Civil rights commissioners would be ordered to investigate the problem. For when it comes to issues of race, there is one set of rules for members of the middle-class elites and another for blue-collar neighborhoods.

During the postwar-era fight over segregation, the people who shouted in heavily accented English and shook their fists at blacks demanding an end to segregation seemed little more than barbarians to the enlightened elements of middle-class Americans who could afford to flee. As the historian Arnold Hirsch notes, nothing would have shocked the residents of Chicago's Gold Coast or Hyde Park (home to the prestigious University of Chicago) "more than the assertion that they were part of a generalized *white* effort to control the process of racial succession in Chicago. The imputation of brotherhood (and sisterhood) with the ethnic, working-class rock throwers would have been more than they could bear. Yet," as Hirsch provocatively points out, "there was just such a consensus. Each of the various white groups or interests agreed on the fundamental undesirability of racial succession. Each of them (social elite and blue collar) were, for their own reasons, unable or unwilling to flee the city, and each believed that the process had to be controlled to protect their self-defined claims. While there was certainly a divergence in the means that were available to manage succession (the elites preferred urban renewal, managed integration, and political expediencies whereas the working class relied on grassroots demonstrations, incendiary rhetoric, and violence), identical fears about living in close proximity to large numbers of poor blacks inspired their action." Although the calls for integration among the politically and socially powerful were in sharp contrast to the racist diatribes voiced by working-class whites in the Bungalow Belt, "the justifications given for actions taken reveal the differences among the various white groups to be more in the vehemence of the language and the sophistication of the resistance than in fundamental assumptions."[11] Working-class whites were looked down upon as ignorant thugs by their middle-class counterparts. To the working-class whites, middle-class whites' calls for integration, on middle-class whites' terms, seemed utterly hypocritical.

In the end, when Civil Rights leaders turned the old racial order on its head, working-class whites were on the front lines. As the old order was dismantled, they were the segment of society most demonized and vilified for their unabashed support for the old ways of conducting racial business in this country. Because working-class whites invested so much in the efforts to defend the old racial order, in the post–Civil Rights era they would pay the highest reparations for being defeated. As Hirsch argues, in the wake of the Civil Rights struggle working-class whites were forced to abandon Englewood and Gage Park while places such as Hyde Park, the Loop, and Lincoln Park thrived as communities for affluent whites and carefully regulated numbers of blacks. As the growing black population burst through the old boundaries of the Black Belt, political strategies, public housing, and economic redevelopment kept black Chicagoans contained in a ghetto that was being reconfigured instead of dismantled. In the end, working-class whites witnessed their cherished neighborhoods get dragged down by the ghetto's devastation.[12] Many of the whites, those that could, ran for the safety of the suburbs or the north, south, and west sections of the Bungalow Belt.

To Chicago's Bungalow Belt working-class white inhabitants, the new world created by civil rights and desegregation made them feel as if they had woken up in the middle of a dream. Why were they the only ones fighting for the way things were and had always been when it came to race in America? The politicians had betrayed them and now blamed "good, decent, and hardworking citizens" like themselves for living by rules that were changed without their knowledge or permission. From the perspective of those living on the front lines of the battles over race, middle-class America had come by its progressive views on race on the cheap. Suburbanites watched Washington, Los Angeles, Boston, Philadelphia, and Chicago burn on the nightly news; middle-class urbanites were not being asked to live down the street from towering housing projects. While the true victims of race in America were, of course, African Americans, working-class whites could legitimately claim that upper-class whites could more easily avoid the costs of racial change. When the fighting had finally come to an end, somehow the residents of the gardens and the ghettoes were the only ones left standing with blood on their hands.

Unlike the residents of working-class enclaves like Chicago's Bridgeport (home to both Mayor Daleys) who chose to stay and fight the racial and class changes facing their community, the working-class residents of the Southwest Side have tended to use flight as their strategy. In these working-class white communities, as neighborhoods and housing stock age and the old-timers move on (through either illness or death), the younger generation often moves just a few blocks west to keep some distance between them and the ghetto. Over time white Bungalow Belt dwellers came to attach a "Maginot Line"–like significance to streets like Kedzie, Western, and Ashland. Each time working-class whites moved further west and south or west and north, the racial "Maginot Line" would move along with them (see Map 1). According to the work of sociologist Eileen McMahon, from 1967 to 1969 more than 2,000 families left white neighborhoods on the South Side of the Bungalow Belt for neighborhoods just to the west, places just like Beltway.

Today, many of Beltway's residents are city workers (police officers, streets and sanitation workers, firefighters, park district employees) who must reside within the city limits as a condition of their employment. Many of these city workers admit that they would prefer to move (places like Orland Park and Tinley Park are frequently mentioned destinations), but attractive suburbs remain costly, unattainable options. Indeed, because there are so few stable, affordable, white working- and lower-middle-class neighborhoods remaining in Chicago, city workers have a strong incentive to maintain the distinctive way of life Beltway provides, for "if Beltway goes, there's no place left to go." The widely held conviction that Beltway cannot easily be replaced makes residents protective of the community, even if they secretly long to escape.[13] Other Beltway dwellers, particularly the older generation, are tied to the neighborhood because of their status as homeowners. The brick bungalows represent the largest single purchase of their lives. Working-class homeowners find that their financial circumstances have become inextricably linked to their neighborhood's future. For many residents, living in one of the brick bungalows makes it possible to afford other luxuries like private school for the kids, a cabin by a lake, an RV, or possibly occasional vacations to Las Vegas and Disneyworld. A move to the suburbs means giving up the little extras. In other cases, a move to the sub-

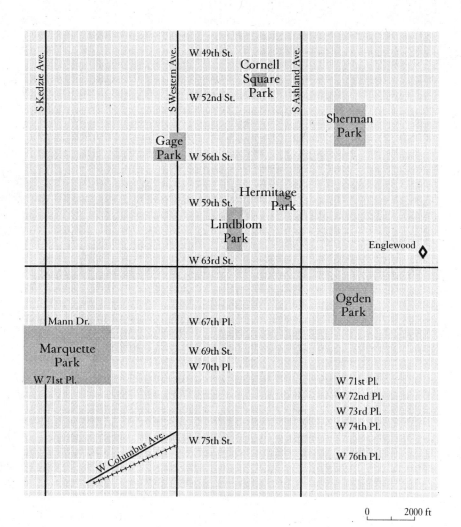

Map 1. The racial "Maginot Line." As Hispanics, Arabs, Asians, and African Americans have moved west through Chicago during the past three decades, the boundary separating the "Bungalow Belt" and the "Black Belt" has moved from Ashland, to Western, and most recently to Kedzie. The data was compiled from *Chicago Community Fact Book: 1990* and the U.S. Census (2000).

urbs simply holds no appeal because it means being far away from friends, family, and familiar routines.

Because Beltwayites cannot or will not flee to the suburbs, local activists must maintain the borders of their community. Residents' obsession with the visual appearance of public and private space, their solicitousness of their homes, their fears about decay and disorder—these shared common values—all serve as weapons in Beltway's symbolic defense. Over and over again, Beltwayites can be heard to evoke the militaristic imagery of the Beltway area as "the last stand."

The "last stand" imagery resonates with young and old alike. In the words of former Alderman John Puchinski, "This area on the Southwest Side and a section of the Northwest Side are really the last two, how shall I say, bastions of neighborhood stability." Puchinski continues, "What is happening is that people who work for the city have to live in the city of Chicago, so I'm getting a lot of younger people...policemen, firemen." Fears about crime and racial turnover have forced working-class whites to abandon sections of the city that were once affordable, safe, stable, working-class, and white. The alderman explains, "There are areas of the city that are changing with high crime rates or the neighborhoods are changing, so to speak, and people are moving either to the Southwest or Northwest Side if they have to stay in the city." In Puchinski's carefully worded description of the Southwest Side, "changing" and "bastions of stability" are loaded terms, code words for the dichotomy of the Haves (or at least the Have-a-Little-Mores) and Have-Nots, the racial divide between white and black, garden and ghetto. Mary Corrigan, a young mother and Chicago police officer who lives in Beltway with her husband Steve, also a Chicago cop, uses more blunt terms to explain the housing conundrum faced by working-class whites and working-class city workers in particular. "My husband and I are city workers and I don't know about you, but we ain't going nowhere, there's no place else to go."

But besides "the last stand," Beltway dwellers have other ways of talking about their corner of Chicago. Residents regularly describe the neighborhood as "beautiful," a "utopia," and most evocatively, "the last garden spot in Chicago." Beltway residents do not mind the smells from the factories, the noise from Midway Airport, or the soot that seems to cover everything. As I heard residents proclaim that their neighborhood—this place—is beautiful, I came to see the Beltway from the viewpoint of its full-time inhabitants. I took note of the elaborate lawn decorations, manicured grass, color-coordinated kitchens, fastidiously cared-for American-made cars, and graffiti-free alleys and streets. Such displays require the solicitous care of local activists and property owners. The people of Beltway willingly dedicate themselves to the care of the neighborhood landscape with an unquestioned, nearly spiritual devotion.

Most people have heard of the famous monikers for Chicago such as the line from writer Carl Sandburg, "city of big shoulders," or "the windy city," a reference to Chicago's colorful political history.[14] Yet the city known for the great fire of 1871 and its stockyards and meat-packing industry has as its official motto "Urbs in Horto" which, translated from Latin, means "City in a Garden." Lifelong Southwest Sider Congressman William Lipinski regularly describes the city neighborhoods of his district as "the last garden spot in Chicago." Congressman Lipinski explains he did not coin the expression himself; "actually it was a fellow by the name of Joe Baraka who was a barber on Archer Avenue." Local residents are indeed devoted to landscaping and gardening. Civic groups such as the Midway Garden Club and the neighborhood Civic League along with the Beltway branch of the Chicago Public Library regularly sponsor activities for local gardeners. Events range from discussions about roses and vegetable gardens to presentations on how to create compost heaps within the environs of the city. Neighbors take great pleasure in showing off their magnificent (if sometimes over-the-top) landscaping efforts.

The notion of the garden also exists on the mythic level of the Garden of Eden. A garden is a place of cultivated order and abundance and, without question, the two things the residents of Beltway want most to cultivate in their lives are order and abundance. Beltway symbolizes an Edenic refuge from the uncertainty and chaos whirling about its working- and lower-middle-class inhabitants. The people of Beltway define and defend their place and identity in American society in the face of the growing threat to their way of life and achievements posed by their physical and social proximity to the ghetto. In the world garden dwellers inhabit, chaos takes a multitude of forms: the ghetto, crime, poverty, abandoned buildings, graffiti, filth, unsupervised kids, gangs, and economic uncertainty. The manicured lawns, cookie-cutter houses, and clean streets transform the neighborhood's visual landscape into an oasis of order. Residents' extreme attention to cleanliness perpetuates order. The bungalow-style housing (clean, boxy, brick), the orderliness of the furnishings, and the high standard for keeping house—all the ritualistic displays of housepride—become declarations of stability and decency, particularly among women. The primordial hunger for order grows out of human beings' endeavors to make sense and meaning out of the world, for radical separation from order and meaning constitutes a fundamental threat to the individual.[15]

Beltway, as a place of abundance, comes to life through the dazzling displays of hospitality and consumption. At family functions such as weddings or graduation parties, food is customarily served "family style," which means massive platters are passed around so the guests may have a choice of three or four entrées. Guests may select from a variety of popular staples including mostaciolli with meat sauce, roast pork, chicken, potatoes, dumplings (or pierogies soaked in butter), and boiled vegetables drenched in mayonnaise dressing. For dessert, kolackis, strudels, bundt cakes, cheesecakes, fruit-filled gelatin molds, fruit ambrosia, and pies will be crammed on to every free inch of table and counter space. The displays of abundance also come to life in Beltway residents' consumption of cars, houses, furniture, and even the way their kids are dressed. Indeed, the inhabitants of Beltway do not simply use their possessions, they care for and display material goods with a nearly religious veneration. In this world, consumption is no passive, empty activity. On the contrary, among the residents of the last garden, consumption represents a serious symbolic and cultural endeavor. The working-class residents of Beltway labor to transform empty physical *space* into a symbolically significant *place* that reinforces and reproduces the values of its working-class inhabitants. A *place* is not simply discovered; people construct it as a practical activity.

Sociologists John Logan and Harvey Molotch write: "Place itself is a social construction.... We do not dispose of place after it is bought and used." A place "holds a particular preciousness to its users[;] even when compared to other items, such as food, place is still distinctive."[16] In a fragile and uncertain world, the collective community-level cultivation of the last garden becomes a philosophy about the meaning of home and the good life.

Beltway is the type of community (and there are a number of others throughout the country such as Philadelphia's Northeast, Milwaukee's South Side neighborhoods, Boston's Hyde Park and the old Irish and Italian sections of Brighton, Baltimore's Hamden, and New York City's Floral Park) that our usual image of inner-city ghettoes and gentrifying neighborhoods misses. In Beltway there is a story about the nature of working-class life, about a particular kind of urbanism, and a segment of the working class that did not join the rush to the suburbs. In Gerald Gamm's historical account of Jews and Catholics in Boston (1999), he argues that the Catholics were more likely to stay in the city because of connections to Catholic parishes versus urban Jews' more flexible ties to their synagogues, and thus attenuated links to their neighborhoods. While parish life[17] is indeed an important facet of life within the neighborhood, there are a variety of reasons that have kept the people of Beltway from fleeing to the suburbs. Given that the dust had settled in the battles for racial turf by the 1990s, most Beltway residents now view fleeing the city as a solution if and only if the streets become unsafe and "the bad neighbors start to outnumber the good ones."

• • •

In order to document the last garden and the people of Beltway's unique sense of place, I adopted the stance of an ethnographer. I have sacrificed breadth for depth in an attempt to capture what it means to live in Beltway in all its subtlety. From 1993 to 1998, my research partner and fellow sociologist (and by 1994, my husband) Patrick Carr and I allowed ourselves to become swept up in Beltway life as much as possible. For much of our research, we relied on participant observation and detailed fieldnotes. We would visit the neighborhood to attend community meetings and local events, hang out at the library, chat over coffee in a kitchen or a local diner, and then go home and write detailed notes of what we had heard and observed. We had first come to Beltway as part of a large multi-neighborhood study sponsored by William Julius Wilson and Richard Taub at the University of Chicago's Center for the Study of Inequality. Wilson and Taub sent Patrick and me to Beltway to look at how a stable, working-/lower-middle-class white neighborhood "gets things done." More precisely, Wilson and Taub examined four stable and viable urban neighborhoods to find out what works there so that they could understand better what does not work in economically disadvantaged inner-city ghetto areas.

Because of Wilson and Taub's intellectual generosity and trust in their student researchers, Pat and I got free rein to move about the community and follow whatever seemed interesting. Admittedly, this very freedom probably resulted in our spending five years in the field. As Gerald Suttles once observed, the two hardest things about fieldwork are getting in, and getting out. Pat and I began our tentative foray into the field by carefully mapping the neighborhood in a car and on foot and reading about the neighborhood in the weekly local newspaper. Eventually, it was the newspaper that offered our first introduction to the people of Beltway when we decided to phone Helen Vidich, the author of the *Southwest News Herald*'s Beltway neighborhood column. Helen's weekly column is sort of a cross between a neighborhood newsletter, society page, and platform for musings on topics ranging from patriotism to lawn care. When we called Helen, she was guarded but still offered to meet with us at her home. She said she would invite her husband Joe and their friend, the current president of the neighborhood Civic League, Ron Zalinsky, a retired foreman for Nabisco. Helen and Joe, a retired electrician, reside in a tidy bungalow located on busy Third Avenue. We were invited to sit in the front living room, a room rarely used for entertaining. In fact, this would be one of the few times we would sit in a living room for an interview. As we came to be known in the neighborhood, most people would host us over coffee and cake around the kitchen table.

Our first trip to Beltway to meet the Vidiches and Ron Zalinsky became a two-hour-long conversation where Joe and Ron (Helen deferred to the more talkative men) talked about the Beltway Civic League, the neighborhood, their families, and local, national, and international politics. In time, we were invited to attend the monthly Civic League meetings held in the basement of the Beltway United Methodist Church. (In fact, we are members of the Civic League to this day. The newsletter still comes to our apartment in Philadelphia.) The meeting proved fortuitous, for once the three decided to vouch for Pat and me, we were welcomed into their immediate circle of acquaintances and friends. Indeed, it is through Civic League meetings that we came to meet many of our most important informants and contacts in the neighborhood.

Soon afterwards, and again with the blessing of the Vidiches and Ron Zalinsky, we were encouraged to contact Lydia Donovan and Stan Hart. Lydia, the head librarian of the Beltway branch of the Chicago Public Library, is a bubbly, intelligent, and fast-talking single mother of a teenage daughter, who found her way to the Southwest Side after growing up in Muncie, Indiana. Lydia, who holds a master's degree in library science, is one of the most well-known activists in the neighborhood. She privately admits that her inspiration for community activism comes from the writings of the radical organizer (and one-time University of Chicago sociology graduate student) Saul Alinsky. Alinsky was widely known in the Southwest Side in the 1960s as the brilliant, charismatic leader of the Back of the Yards Neighborhood Association. He eventually, however, became persona non grata to many white working-class Chicagoans when he supported efforts calling for desegregation. It was Lydia who lent Pat and me her worn paperback copy of *Rules for Radicals*.

A former president of the Civic League, Lydia became one of our key informants. She, more than any other Beltway resident, probably had the best sense of what Patrick and I hoped to accomplish in our research. As a librarian and former resident of Muncie, she was quite familiar with the Lynds' classic ethnographic study of that town titled *Middletown*. Moreover, while Lydia is quite respected and admired for her work in the neighborhood, she has adopted the Southwest Side as her home. She is not a native Beltwayite, and as such, she was an ideal informant for she could move freely within Beltway society and serve as our guide within the community while still maintaining her own more critical gaze as someone who is not truly "from" the neighborhood.

Stan Hart, a retired plumber who served in Korea, is a descendant of one of the first families to settle Beltway in the early 1900s. Hart has such affection for the Beltway neighborhood that he wrote (and published) a book on its history. In fact, on more than one occasion, when I told people in Beltway I was writing a book about the neighborhood, they would respond matter-of-factly, "Did you know Stan Hart already wrote one?" When Stan heard that Patrick and I were interested in learning about the neighborhood's history, he graciously offered to take us on a tour of "old" Beltway. His book and conversations with us served as a wonderful foundation for this contemporary study of the neighborhood. Indeed, the fact that we had spoken to "Bear" (as he is known to many in the neighborhood because of his towering lumberjack build) opened up many doors to us in the process of our research. It would be impossible to write about Beltway without talking to Stan Hart.

As I stated earlier, our first contact with a neighborhood organization came through the Beltway Civic League. The group was founded in 1960 when local women protested against a zoning ordinance petition to expand the facilities of a chemical factory into a densely populated residential section of the neighborhood. At the first Civic League meeting we attended, Patrick and I had very purposefully seated ourselves at the far back of the church's basement hall. Ron Zalinsky, the gravel-voiced Civic League president who has run the organization since the 1980s and has been active with the group since the '60s, pounded his gavel to call the meeting to order. He then insisted that we stand up and tell the group all about ourselves and our project. Patrick fumbled through an awkward introduction and explained how we were interested in finding out about the neighborhood and "how the neighborhood gets things done." The 20 or so residents (mostly in their sixties and seventies) silently took in what we had to say. At the end of the meeting, several people came up to introduce themselves and share their opinions about a variety of subjects.

Ron later made the slight faux pas of introducing me as Pat's secretary.[18] This misunderstanding was one we were quick to take advantage of: Pat would be the more talkative "man" and I would be the quiet "woman" assisting him in his work. No doubt, my presence as a woman, and later a wife, made our attendance at meetings and events less threatening and, ultimately, less strange. My gender also gave us a practical advantage in our fieldwork since we would split up and "work a room" along the naturally occurring lines of gender segregation. I would go off to chat with the women preparing food in the kitchen, and Pat would pass his time sipping coffee with the men holding court in another part of the room.

Over time, we were known as the students from the University of Chicago, an affiliation we were careful to downplay because for many white Southwest Siders the university was infamous as a hotbed of radical integrationist politics. On one of those early visits to the neighborhood, Stan Hart joked that "he had never met communists before." On another occasion, we were introduced to a local cop who had also served in Vietnam. The police officer resided in Beltway with his wife and four kids. When he heard about our connection to the university he eyed us warily as he recalled the University of Chicago's explosive student demonstrations. For the most part, however, the people of Beltway welcomed us into their lives and their homes. If someone they knew and trusted had vouched for us through an introduction, no one would question our presence. Throughout our years in the neighborhood, there were only two occasions when people refused to speak to us or questioned our right to be there. In one instance, one of the local parish priests repeatedly declined our requests to be interviewed. In another case, when we attended a Local School Council (LSC) meeting—open to the public—the council members demanded to know if we had children at the school. Eventually, we learned that their apprehensiveness had less to do with us as researchers and more to do with the growing swell of community opposition to the manner in which they governed the council. Some months later, this very same council was dissolved by Chicago Public Schools CEO Paul Vallas after dozens of local parents organized a neighborhood-wide petition drive and letter-writing campaign to protest the LSC leadership's gross abuses of power. For the most part, the people of Beltway seemed quite flattered that Patrick and I had chosen to write books about the neighborhood. Over the years, some of our friends hoped we would move to the neighborhood permanently. We came to be known as "the Carrs" (I never corrected anyone when they referred to me by my married name), "Pat and Maria," or the "people writing the book."

While Pat went on to write about the community responses to crime, I decided to focus on how the people of Beltway inscribe the world they inhabit with meaning through a particular sense of place. In the beginning years of the research, I relied on fieldnotes and participant observation almost exclusively. Much of my data comes from the physical appearance of the neighborhood itself (the display of flags, the appearance of the houses, and the perfectly manicured lawns). I excavated the objects of everyday life to understand how the residents of Beltway make sense and meaning of the world they inhabit. By the end of the project, I was conducting in-depth personal interviews recorded on audiotape.

Almost all the events I describe in the book I observed firsthand, and I supplemented much of my research with newspaper accounts of local events from 1993 to 1998.

Throughout the five-year project, Patrick and I lived in Hyde Park (the South Side neighborhood where the University of Chicago is located), just a few miles east of Beltway. Many of our friends came to our home in Hyde Park, and we socialized a great deal with people in the neighborhood. Our proximity to the neighborhood made fieldwork convenient. At the same time, living in Hyde Park surrounded by the university community created a buffer zone that protected us from the dangers of going native. I also believe that living close by to (but not in) the community we were writing about helped us keep a critical distance. Our drives back to Hyde Park were invariably filled with heated conversations dissecting what we had seen, heard, and done on our visit to the neighborhood. We parlayed our contacts through the Civic League into interviews with "key informants" such as school principals, priests, a minister, police officers, and various politicians. Over time, we moved beyond such formal and institutional contacts to the more informal and intimate networks within the community. In the five years we conducted fieldwork, we worked political campaigns, went to dozens of community meetings, volunteered in a summer camp at a local park, attended birthday and graduation celebrations, chaperoned school field trips, helped out on a church camping trip for neighborhood youngsters, went to church, and baked cookies. I ate brats (bratwurst) (because Pat is a vegetarian), Pat drank beer (because I rarely drink), and we both drank lots of pop and coffee and consumed lots of kolackis, coffee cakes, pierogies, and mostaciolli.

My most sustained and richest contacts with the neighborhood came through a group called the bunco squad. A group of mothers (and one grandmother) from the Hastings School socialized once a month, taking turns to entertain the group of about dozen women with bunco parties. Bunco is a gambling dice game and a strictly enforced women only (i.e., no kids, no men) affair. Husbands were exiled from the house for the evening and kids were sent off to bed. Each of the guests brought chips, dips, and assorted junk food snacks. The hostess provided pop and her kitchen or basement family room. These evenings were opportunities to gossip, get bawdy and raunchy, de-brief, complain, and maybe escape from the daily grind of work, family, and marriage. At these gatherings women opened a window into the viewpoints and experiences of decent, hardworking, working- and lower-middle-class women with children.

A cautionary word may help the reader make sense of the book. In the course of my time in Beltway, I had to make choices about the people and places I could visit. Because of my initial focus on social organization, my primary contacts were with individuals most active in community groups and civic life. To a large extent, a disproportionate amount of my time was spent with people who embrace the values of the last garden. Clearly, there are those who resist the safe and restrictive world the people of Beltway inhabit. Beltway is probably not the easiest place to live if you are gay, poor, neither working- nor lower-middle-class, overly educated, unmarried, or not Catholic. Not "fitting in" in Beltway can make life there complicated, if not downright uncomfortable. Yet, over the five years I spent in Beltway, I did come to know people who lived on the outskirts of the last garden's value system. If they had lawns that were overgrown or houses that were not decorated with color-coordinated curtains and upholstery, these people were certainly cognizant of how their choices represented a rejection of the values most of their neighbors chose to embrace. Some residents would joke about how not having a well-maintained home made them seem more "white trash" than their neighbors.[19] For others, the overgrown lawns were a means of exacting their private revenge on the controlling way of life the garden represents. In some instances, people were terrified to let others into their homes for fear their neighbors would think less of them for "how my house is." However, whether one embraces or reviles the values of the last garden, all the people of Beltway are no doubt aware of the rules that govern life there. More important, people are drawn to the garden because this strictly enforced sense of place makes them feel safe, comfortable, and reassured that the danger and chaos of the ghettoes just to the east will not engulf them.

◆　　◆　　◆

Chapter One, titled "Rethinking Race in the Ethnic White Enclave," provides a brief history of Beltway including an overview of the demographic, social, and racial transformations in the neighborhood and the city of Chicago as a whole. Chronicling the racial hostilities that crystallized most outsiders' impressions of what it means to live in a defended working-class urban neighborhood like Beltway will serve as the starting point for this account of life in working-class Chicago. To maintain the idea that places such as Beltway are inhabited solely by satirical caricatures, Archie Bunker–like figures who refuse to accept the social transformations of the last 40 years, is to gloss over a powerful and important segment of the American population. People living in places like Beltway regularly vote in presidential elections, pay their taxes, work hard to care for their families, purchase homes, cars, and other consumer goods, and, most important, believe that they represent the moral core of American society.

Chapter Two, "A Precious Corner of the World," documents how place, on the level of the neighborhood, reflects and reinforces Beltwayites' understanding of their social location in the world. The neighborhood's sense of place is a possession that neighbors may claim through their efforts and labors to keep Beltway "as best they can." And Beltway, as the last garden spot in Chicago sitting on the edge of the ghetto, is a place that must be protected from the destructive forces of decay, disorder, filth, poverty, and crime. Beltwayites' fears about graffiti and crime are not merely expressions of racism; rather, they reflect residents' insecurities about holding on to the appearance of order, abundance, and respectability they have worked so hard to cultivate. On one level, battles over segregation have scarred working-class Chicagoans. Past experiences make Beltway residents fearful about sharing their community with people who are different. At the same time, practical realities and the victories of the Civil Rights era compel Beltwayites to see beyond the old racial order. While racial animosities persist, Beltwayites appear more willing than ever before to make their community open to people of color. Such newcomers will be welcomed—or at least tolerated—as long as they join the fight against crime and chaos. The case of Orlando Santos, a neighborhood teenager caught vandalizing the windows of a local elementary school, shows how race, class, and place collide in residents' current endeavors to protect the neighborhood and its distinctive way of life. The deaths of Teresa Powell and Melissa Harvey, two 13-year-old girls from the neighborhood who were shot by local teenagers, illustrate the irony of how residents' ongoing efforts to maintain the visual landscape mask the symptoms of homegrown problems Beltwayites customarily associate with the ghetto and low-income minority populations.

In Chapter Three, "Home, Sweet Home," I use thick description to show how Beltway's working-class residents, in particular women, use the appearance of their homes and property to make sincere and powerful declarations about self. Home-ownership is not just an economically relevant activity; it also has cultural and symbolic elements that play important roles in working-class Beltwayites' social performances and their ideas about identity, status, and moral worth. Moreover, just as they do on the level of the neighborhood, Beltwayites use the ordered, self-conscious household displays as talismans to protect their way of life from the destructive social forces that undermine their claims to respectability and stability.

Chapter Four, "For Country and Home," explores the nested relationships between hearth and home, neighborhood and nation. Memorial Day services for area veterans, celebrations of patriotism through displays of flags and recitations of the Pledge of Allegiance, and even displaying POW/MIA bumper stickers make the nation come to life on the *local* level for Beltway's garden dwellers. Recent history with wars in Vietnam and the Persian Gulf have taught Beltwayites to be cynical about the motives of politicians who are so willing to send "our boys" to fight for nebulous corporate interests and political strategy. Instead, the people of Beltway believe that the real America exists in the lives of ordinary citizens such as themselves. Veterans insist they were not fighting for political ideologues, they were fighting to guard their right "to the pursuit of happiness" and "to return home to their families and homes" in places like Beltway. The people of Beltway also proudly declare they are American, without double-barreled disclaimers like "Mexican American" or "Italian American," for being American is to move beyond the poverty of immigrant forbears. Beltwayites believe they earn their status as Americans through hard work, sacrifice, morality, love of country, and caring for home, family, and community.

In the Conclusion, I review how the story of Beltway instructs us about class, culture, race and ethnicity, and community in the postindustrial city of the post–Civil Rights era. Ultimately, what the people of Beltway would mourn the loss of if "the garden" ceased to exist is a distinctive sense of place that reinforces the values residents use to make meaning and order in their everyday lives.

◆　　◆　　◆

At one point while I was writing this book a professor friend who grew up in a working-class Northwest Side neighborhood "not quite as nice as" Beltway mused (with genuine concern) that the book might become a handbook for cynical politicians to tap into the populist resentment of the white working class. While I am pleased that anyone, in particular nonsociologists, might be interested in purchasing this book, my purpose in writing it is neither to lobby for a particular constituency nor to ridicule a segment of the population. As an ethnographer and a scholar, I aim to explain sociologically how the people of Beltway make sense of the world they inhabit and cultivate a sense of place that embodies their values about the home, the neighborhood, and the nation. If, in the process of hearing this story, the reader comes to empathize with the people in the book, I am optimistic that this understanding will give us insight into a group of people who are too often simplistically dismissed as racist and parochial. By coming to terms with what the last garden's dwellers cherish and want to protect, one can explain sociologically how white Beltwayites came to feel the way they do about matters that have powerful social and political implications. I can only hope that this knowledge will help improve relations among all city dwellers, but particularly the ones living in the gardens and the ghettoes.

The fact that I have tried to inject as little of myself as possible into this narrative may leave some readers with the impression that I have sided with the interests of urban "whites" fearful about poverty, crime, and racial turnover. Others may be pained about how I have portrayed the people of Beltway. They may accuse me of being a bourgeois, elitist intellectual who is ridiculing the people I describe. Neither one of these interpretations is correct. It is my wish that this book will serve as a map, of sorts, to the last garden's cultural landscape.

ONE

Rethinking Race
in the Ethnic White Enclave

A NEIGHBORHOOD HISTORY: 1910 TO 1960

Farmers first settled the area that would come to be known as Beltway in the early 1900s. This unnamed section of prairie just beyond the city limits was little more than a sleepy hamlet. In time, this small farming community would become a mud-covered company town for local railway yards. By 1915, the City of Chicago annexed Beltway. Beltway's clearing yards for the railroad—vast, oval-shaped switching yards for loading and unloading freight—would become one of the city's major railway transport centers. As the railroad industry grew, so too did the railway yard owners' demand for laborers. Thousands of workers were needed to keep up with the freight moving in and out of a sprawling young Chicago. Eager to attract families to settle in Beltway, area industrialists subsidized the construction of roads, water and sewage lines, and housing. Fearing that Beltway would become yet another rough and tumble railroad boomtown, they used zoning regulations to restrict the construction of saloons, speakeasies, and other less respectable businesses. Members of the Beltway Industrial District (a consortium of local business owners) envisioned a plan to build a "model" residential community for workers. Beltway remained a hardworking farming and railroading community until the 1950s.

By the end of World War I, Midway Airport dramatically transformed the face of Beltway. The first wave of mass-produced workingmen's housing was constructed in the 1920s. The neighborhood's population doubled in the decade between 1920 and 1930. Sturdy brick bungalows[1] replaced the old wooden-framed farmhouses. Local industry grew at a phenomenal rate. From 1918 to 1928, the number of factories in the Beltway Industrial District increased fivefold.[2] With the onset of the Great Depression, industrial growth in the area surrounding Beltway came to a complete standstill. Yet even during this period of economic stagnation, local factories still played a prominent role in the day-to-day lives of the surrounding neighborhood and its inhabitants. When panicked depositors ran the Beltway branch of the Illinois Bank during the crash of 1929, local business leaders saved the day by rescuing the bank with a $100,000 cash payment.

Beltway, once populated solely by farmers and small business owners, was now home to ever-growing numbers of European immigrants. Most of these new arrivals from Germany, Italy, Lithuania, and Poland had come to take the jobs as laborers in the factories. By the 1930 Census, almost one-quarter of Beltway's population was foreign born. The descendants of the pioneer farmers and the new arrivals from Europe were cordial neighbors by all accounts. In the years before and after Prohibition, local people enjoyed sharing their secrets for making German and Dutch homebrews and homemade Italian wines. "The art (of wine and beer making) spread quickly to folks of all heritages," recalls local historian Stan Hart. "Now Beltway was never an ethnic neighborhood as so many others were. If you got along with your neighbors, were a hard worker or could play baseball, that's all that mattered."

In time, the war effort in Europe reawakened Beltway's local industry. Midway Airport became one of the busiest airports in the world, and Beltway's local populace was thoroughly working-class. Over 95 percent of the neighborhood's workers held traditional blue- and pink-collar jobs. To house workers for an engineering plant central to the war effort, the government ordered the construction of a housing development in the eastern section of Beltway. The "Ford Village" would be a mixture of single- and multi- family dwellings. Even though the Village's residents were to be employed at the government plant, locals feared that the complex would attract a lower-class element to the area. The physical design of the development seems "to have been built for isolation rather than integration into the community."[3] A number of access roads in the Village were dead ends. The elliptical layout of the housing development makes the roads confusing and difficult to navigate. Local historian Stan Hart explains, "The traditional welcoming of new Beltwayites to make them feel at home was impossible because of the sudden sheer weight of numbers and the project's isolated design." He goes on to say that the development's "isolated design, the initial resistance to it, the thought that it might become a slum and the lack of gradual integration" turned Columbia Avenue into a symbolic boundary dividing the residents of east Beltway from their slightly "better off" neighbors to the west.[4] This distinction lingers to this day.

By the 1950s, a nationwide housing boom fueled the wildfire development of Beltway. The neighborhood's population swelled by almost three-quarters from 1940 to 1950. Generous mortgage relief programs and a bountiful economy made returning GIs long for homes for young, growing families. To meet the incredible housing demand, developers raced to construct hundreds of new bungalows[5] on the neighborhood's acres of undeveloped prairie land. The rows of neat little box bungalow—style houses engulfed the landscape and gave Beltway a sleek, if routinized, suburban feel. The "company town" became, practically overnight, an expanse of nearly identical one-story brick houses. Stan Hart remembers returning home from the Korean War to bear witness to the neighborhood's momentous metamorphosis in just two years. "When I'd left there'd been prairie land out here, by the time I got back, all you could see was those bungalows."

As children of European immigrants steadily replaced the old "pioneer" stock farmers, the Poles, Lithuanians, Germans, Italians, and Irish changed the face of neighborhood.[6] Most of the newcomers were Catholic, and the growing Catholic parishes (St. Martin's and St. Bernadette's) quickly became vibrant centers of local life. At the same time, it was a neighborhood about as wide in its job base as in its ethnicity.

Chicago's Southwest Side was no one-industry town. The people of Beltway were policemen and "firemen, pipefitters and steamfitters, workers in the railway yards and at nearby Midway Airport. And they worked in the factories that had given the Southwest Side a self-image as 'the candy capital of the world'—Kool-Aid, Cracker Jack, Tootsie Roll—and Nabisco at 73rd and Kedzie where more than 2000 people turned out Oreos and Mallomars, chocolate chips and Lorna Doones."[7] For those who remembered the stockyards, the smell of the bakeries was a welcome change. "Most of the jobs were hard physical jobs, and some of them were semi-skilled, but they produced middle-class family living. 'They were really clean jobs for factories,' one of the children of the Southwest Side remembers. 'My mom would come home smelling like Kool-Aid. All you had in the air at Kool-Aid was sugar dust.'"[8]

The "Bungalow Belt" quickly came to symbolize ethnic white Chicago's version of the American Dream. In the old neighborhoods, many families had lived in two-flats, old brick buildings with one apartment upstairs and one downstairs, and sometimes a third living space in the basement. "Often," notes Alan Ehrenhalt, "such buildings housed entire extended families with half a dozen people putting their wages into the mortgage; sometimes, the family that bought the place rented out both upper flats, lived in the basement, and used the double rent to make a monthly payment. The move to a Southwest Side bungalow was a move away from all that—away from uncles and cousins under the same roof, away from having to cater to renters, away from the immigrant experience in general. It was a move to a one-family house, with at most a widowed parent or in-law in residence. It was a move to a home where you didn't have to worry so much about the noise your children were making, or the noise someone else's children were making upstairs."[9]

Owning a Chicago-style bungalow embodied success, security, and achievement.[10] Moving to one of the modern, two or three bedroom, single-family houses meant you had made it. But whether you had come to Beltway from Sicily or you had descended from the pioneer families that first farmed the prairie, the people of Beltway took great pride in the nation. It was a time when every house on every block seemed to fly the American flag.

CIVIL RIGHTS AND THE DECLINE OF MANUFACTURING: BELTWAY, 1960 TO 1980

Economic and political fault lines would tear apart white working-class Chicago's taken-for-granted racial status quo by the 1960s. Chicago's mammoth manufacturing industrial complex began to show the earliest symptoms of decline. From 1960 to 1970, the proportion of Beltway residents employed in traditional blue-collar occupations fell nearly 10 percent. Increasingly, Beltway residents found employment in service sector jobs. Beltwayites' collars were now less likely to be blue, and more likely to be pink and white (even if these jobs were on the lowest end of the expanding service sector) (see Table 1).

In the struggles for civil rights and racial equality, school desegregation initiatives and Dr. Martin Luther King's historic marches through the streets of Chicago left the inhabitants of ethnic white strongholds shaken to the core (see Maps 2 and 3). The Beltway Civic League's leadership became loud, unwavering voices in the opposition to bussing and housing desegregation initiatives. When race riots erupted at nearby Carver Heights High School, the threat of violence became so serious that the governor of

TABLE I   1990 LABOR FORCE COMPOSITION

Occupation	Percentage of Beltway Population
Technical/clerical	36.3
Service	14.7
Managerial/professional	16.4
Operators/craftsmen	31.6
Other	1.0

NOTE: Beltway remains solidly blue and pink collar.

Illinois ordered National Guard troops to patrol the school's corridors. Officials eventually shut down the campus in a last, desperate effort to relieve escalating racial tensions. In the days preceding and following the National Guard's takeover, dozens of students were detained and arrested. Local news accounts at the time reported that a group of white teenagers from the neighborhood organized to protect themselves in the wake of the clashes. At a time when the generation gap was a yawning chasm separating young and old in American society, this student "group" (known as the 18th Street Jungle) found a surprising ally in the Beltway Civic League. A May 14, 1970, *Southwest News Herald* story provides an account of a public meeting that was unusual because both young and old gathered to discuss the situation at the high school. At one point during the meeting, a member of the "Jungle" told members of the Civic League and other community residents, "You've probably heard some bad things about our organization, but we're at least trying to protect our way of life." Harry Frank, then president of the Beltway Civic League, declared his unwavering support for the young Jungle members' vigilantism. In an extraordinary statement, Frank, a Chicago firefighter, told the crowd, "I'm preaching law and order now, but if my faith in the government isn't borne out, I'll lead [members of the 18th Street Jungle] in the counterattack." Some three decades later, this violence is etched in the memories of residents.

Harry Frank's wife Ethel was known to share her husband's strident anti-desegregation views. In her testimony at a 1970 Illinois State House of Representatives hearing on fair housing laws, Mrs. Frank stated, "I am speaking for all the people in our community that are on the same level as myself. We are afraid of such laws as HB257 and any other housing bill that may be passed." Mrs. Frank continued, "We worked hard for a place in our community and society. We worked to earn our property, Constitution, and civil rights, as well as belong to a circle in society of our own choosing." In 1972, local activists held one of the largest demonstrations in the community's history. Over 500 neighborhood residents attended the rally to *oppose* the construction of a new pool facility. A former park official says that residents were afraid a pool would attract "undesirables" into the neighborhood. "You see," the man explains in a lowered voice "people in the neighborhood didn't want blacks from Mountain Ridge coming over here."[11]

Much of the angry response to civil rights and desegregation also came from working-class whites' conviction that the government had simply gone too far when it called for integration in schools and residential areas. The government wanted to legislate how regular, hard-working Americans should live in their homes and neighborhoods. As many Southwest Siders were quick to point out, the battles were not changing the schools for the children of the wealthy and powerful. Why should the government create a policy to benefit African Americans solely? American democracy is meant to give everyone an equal opportunity. To working-class whites, civil rights was helping poor blacks by eroding the few hard-won privileges working-class whites could claim. For Lillian Crimmins, the former wife of a Chicago cop who grew up in the Southwest Side, there is no question civil rights' time had come. But, as a young wife and mother watching the battles over bussing and housing engulf her neighborhood throughout the Civil Rights era, she could not help but be angry about how the burden of change was being placed squarely on the backs of Bungalow Belt dwellers. She recalls, "I remember watching the [civil rights] marchers come to the Southwest Side. And I remember people saying, and I remember thinking, here

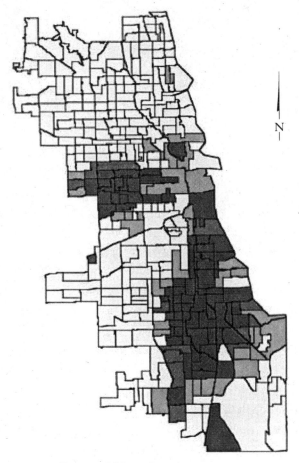

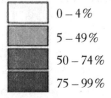

Percent African American

0 – 4%

5 – 49%

50 – 74%

75 – 99%

Map 2. The African American racial composition of Chicago, 1970. Adapted from original map by Jeffrey Morenoff.

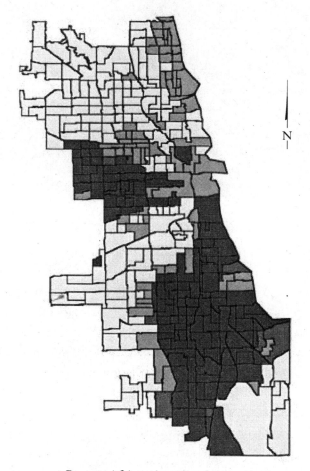

Percent African American

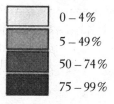

0 – 4%

5 – 49%

50 – 74%

75 – 99%

Map 3.   The African American racial composition of
Chicago, 1990. Adapted from original map by Jeffrey
Morenoff.

we are keeping our neighborhood and following the rules, living our lives. We're not hurting anyone and these people from the University of Chicago and Martin Luther King...were telling us how to live our lives." She insists, "Now I agreed with what Dr. King was saying...but then here were people coming to our homes and our neighborhoods telling us we had to change things. Then it was our boys who were the first to be called up for every war."

WORKING-CLASS WHITE ETHNICS AND WHITE PRIVILEGE

Historian Arnold Hirsch notes, "the notion that Chicago neighborhoods should be defended as if they were ancestral homes may seem incongruous coming, as it did, from people who were residents here for perhaps fewer than two or three or generations. Yet, there was something to it."[12] Many of these working-class areas where residents feared racial succession were neighborhoods that were brought into being by groups who found their traditional insularity disrupted by one of the great population movements of the twentieth century, the Great Migration. "If the neighborhoods' founders, as individuals, were no longer present, there was at least a lasting sense of distinctive community. As trying as the immigrants' ordeal was—one must keep in mind that in the postwar era Chicago's ethnic whites were only a generation removed from the bitter and humiliating struggles against Prohibition, immigration restriction, and other nativistic assaults—by the 1950s working-class white ethnics had largely achieved a certain stability. First, came 'bread and home' and with that had come a modicum of economic security. Second, and especially important after being seared by the brand of racial inferiority in the 1920s, was their newly achieved status as whites." Racial succession, from the standpoint of the working-class white ethnics, challenged both. Threats to their homes, the "respectability" of their communities, or their own precarious status as whites were thus capable of provoking serious violence.[13] Shared experiences, values, and color all led to a common frame of reference among Chicago's white ethnics in interpreting the meaning of neighborhood change and racial turnover.[14] Hirsch continues:

> Ultimately though, the ethnics' defensive yet militant espousal of their *whiteness,* and the demand for privilege on that basis, proved a flawed defense in the context of race relations. First, their assertion of what they held in common with majority society, and the acceptance of that assertion, led, by the 1950s, to their invisibility. When the United Councils of the Polish Roman Catholic Union requested the Polish community in Chicago be represented on the board of the Metropolitan Housing and Planning Council, the MHPC replied that it did not recognize "national" groups as such, but only individuals or groups having interest in housing.... Having become white, ethnic interests merited no distinct consideration. Complacent observers also assumed the luxury of benignly comparing the immigrant and black experiences to the detriment of both. Not only was the immigrant/black analogy cavalier in its assessment of the impediments imposed by color (Saul Alinsky felt the concept was "unfortunate in that it induces a sedative effect, when the situation calls for intrepid, aggressive action"), but it took for granted the eventual integration of the latter into American society on the basis of the former's experience. In so doing, the theory assumed that the immigrants' struggle had been successfully concluded. In presuming that the immigrants—or their descendants, the "ethnics"—had been fully assimilated, the immigrant/black analogy accomplished in a single stroke what was only haltingly, painfully, and often incompletely done. More, it dismissed the experience of working-class white ethnics as unimportant and made their reactions seem simply pathological, the tortured products of the more "backward" elements of a monolithic "white" population. Unlike the middle-class elites and intellectuals (who went to great lengths to demonstrate their sincere motivations and benign intentions), or the blacks now caught in the midst of the conflict, working-class whites, the children and the grandchildren of the men and women who had

suffered so much in the factories, slums, and stockyards, were granted neither the complexity, nor even the significance, of their own history.[15]

Segregation and institutional racism had always placed white ethnics ahead of African Americans in American society, and working-class whites had fiercely guarded those advantages. However, at the very moment that the civil rights movement's victories caused the balance of power to shift, the decline of manufacturing industries in the United State left working-class whites and blacks locked in mortal combat for the few living-wage jobs in manufacturing and industry that remained. In the face of deindustrialization and the recessions of the 1970s, 1980s, and in the early 1990s, working-class whites' racial privilege, social networks, and comparative affluence sheltered them from the economic downturns that devastated working-class blacks.

Poor and working-class blacks who could not afford to flee to suburbs in search of better jobs and better neighborhoods were drawn into the ghetto's destruction. Segregation and concentrated poverty left black inner-city ghettoes acutely vulnerable to economic shifts. As well-paying factory work disappeared, working-class blacks' road to social mobility was blocked. It was true that now working-class whites and blacks shared their schools, jobs, and even political power in ways that had never happened before given the reforms of desegregation and bussing. However, working-class whites' social, economic, and physical proximity to African Americans meant that the gains of working-class and poor blacks put them in direct conflict with working-class whites for precious, limited resources.

Even though working-class whites had fared better economically in the postindustrial era than poor blacks, working-class whites had suffered their own casualties. Service sector jobs of late capitalism could not offer the same union protections, benefits, pensions, and wages of the old industrial-era factory work. In the modern global economy, an economic downturn in Asia leads to a recession in the United States. Under such circumstances, firms usually choose the bottom line over jobs when deciding how to keep competitive. More important, real wages have not seen increases since the 1970s and employees compensate by using overtime and taking second or third jobs. So for all of working-class whites' efforts and sacrifice, they still find that they can be dragged down, maybe not as far and fast as poor blacks, but there could be no question that working- and lower-middle-class whites were running faster and harder just to stay in the same place. More troubling was the fact that for the first time in a century, the belief that one's children would have a better life than their parents no longer seemed to be an assumption that a working-class mother or father could make. Indeed, working-class whites' growing economic precariousness leaves families very susceptible to the risks of teenage pregnancy, violence, drugs, alcoholism, family disruption, and gangs. Such social ills have well-documented links to economic inequality. Under such unsettled conditions, the working- and lower-middle classes find respectability and security all the more elusive.

AFTER THE DUST SETTLED: RACE, CLASS, AND PLACE IN BELTWAY IN THE POST–CIVIL RIGHTS ERA

Every Beltway resident has a story about the neighborhood he, she, family members, or friends were forced to leave behind. Grandmother Peggy Braddock is a warm and expressive woman who stays active in the local Methodist church.[16] Her husband George can trace his family's arrival in Beltway back to the 1900s when farmers settled the prairie. Peggy takes great pride in the fact that she has many African American friends through her church work. While she is critical of her neighbors' and friends' fears about sharing the neighborhood with blacks, she also understands how these fears came to be. Peggy recalls, "We had one Pastor, he was a very nice man but he wanted to leave us because [of what happened] when he wanted to invite people from [the projects] to come to our church. Some of the members were real stiff about that.... One woman [from the church] said, 'You know Pastor, I know you think badly of us, but some of us started out by the lakefront, and we've been pushed and pushed. There's no place to go after here. We're not going to "git" anymore.'"

Today, most white Beltwayites would never consider sending their children to Carver Heights High School, the site of the infamous race riots in 1970. Beltway residents no longer see Carver Heights as a neighborhood school. Indeed, the school has had a highly adversarial relationship with the Beltway neighborhood in recent years. Residents often complain about gang activity and the large numbers of students loitering at bus stops and local businesses after school hours. Parents of Carver Heights students contend that neighborhood residents single out students because of the school's largely minority population. They argue that African American and Hispanic faces are simply not welcome in Beltway. Residents say that no one wants hundreds of teenagers—some of whom may have gang connections—cutting across lawns and back alleys, loitering on corners, getting into fights, and otherwise causing trouble. This is the kind of conflict that epitomizes the nature of neighborhood race relations for Beltway's working-class residents today.

The racial anxiety that enveloped Beltway during the Civil Rights era ended in an anticlimactic stalemate. Large numbers of African Americans never settled in Beltway. Chicago neighborhoods such as Chatham, Beverly, Hyde Park, and Avalon Park and the suburbs ultimately proved more attractive destinations. It was not until the 1980s that Beltway began to face racial integration. In the end, it was not African Americans but Mexicans whose arrival would transform the neighborhood's ethnic and racial landscape. Until 1980, Beltway was 98 percent white. By 1990, the white population had fallen to 92 percent. According to the 2000 Census, Beltway is almost 77 percent white (see Table 2). As older white homeowners were dying off or moving out when they could no longer care for their homes, Hispanic homebuyers replenished whites' declining numbers.[17] Mexicans, the most recent wave of immigrants to settle in Chicago, worked and saved so they could follow in the footsteps of the Irish, Poles, and Italians who came before

TABLE 2   DEMOGRAPHIC BREAKDOWN
OF BELTWAY RESIDENTS

	1960	1970	1980	1990	2000
Adults, 18 years and older (%)	61	63	73	79	77
Minors, 18 years and younger (%)	39	37	27	21	23
Neighborhood racial composition (%)					
Caucasian	100	100	98	91.73	76.34
Black	0	0	0	0.04	0.61
Hispanic	0	0	2	7.52	20.99
Asian	0	0	0	0.55	0.68
Other	0	0	0	0.17	1.38
Total population	18,797	24,911	22,584	21,490	22,331

them.[18] The time had come for Mexicans to move up and out from the crowded two- and three-flats into the sweet little brick bungalows.

Even though open hostilities between working-class whites and blacks have ended, the racially charged battles and social transformations of the 1960s have become hardwired into white Beltwayites' very definition of community. For Toni Capelevski, it is her father's experiences in his once predominantly Irish neighborhood that make her concerned for Beltway's future: "Now my father's neighborhood is still decent, but there have been gunshots. My father built up a wrought iron fence around his house." Toni believes it is the older (white) residents like her father who keep the neighborhood "decent." But she fears, "Once a few of these older people die and they sell their house, his neighborhood is going to be gone." If the same thing were to happen in Beltway, Toni says, "I think [that] would make me move. I would want to stay [here] as long as I could." According to Ava Conrad, a local businesswoman, mother of four, and wife of a Chicago police officer, "Beltway has been fortified as the last garden spot in Chicago."

Race and racism make whites of all ages equate "bad neighbors" with the categories poor and black. Yet if we set race and racism aside, working-class whites who saw stable neighborhoods with high rates of home-ownership metamorphose into high poverty areas with transient renters can rightly say their old neighborhoods have changed for the worse. No one wants to live in the ghetto, least of all the people who are trapped there. Anyone with the opportunity and the means to leave will most likely choose to do so. The problem arises when working-class whites fail to acknowledge how their own fear and racism contribute to the demise of "stable" neighborhoods. As Jonathan Rieder writes, "Racial tipping is a self-fulfilling prophecy, the outcome of white susceptibility to superstition more than an inherent dynamic of integration. Whites displaced their anxieties onto blacks and the stampede that resulted was touched off by white fear."[19] The fact that whites ran so fast is what destabilized communities during the crucial period of the transition from white to black. If neighbors had not panicked at the first sign of black faces moving in next door, housing prices might not have collapsed. The socioeconomic composition of these neighborhoods would not necessarily have shifted from working-class to poor. It is possible that many neighborhoods could have been saved from becoming more burned-out blocks of the ghetto.

Working-class whites often fail to acknowledge the complex processes that contributed to the decline of neighborhoods. It is not simply that blacks arrived and the neighborhood went down. A constellation of forces (namely suburbanization, globalization, segregation, and deindustrialization) destroyed America's inner cities. But what working-class whites believe is that the arrival of blacks sounded a death knell for good, solid, and respectable neighborhoods. As one Beltway resident in his sixties states, "Of course there are good blacks, blacks that want things that are better for themselves and their families. But even blacks don't want the bad ones living around them." The younger generation is more accustomed to sharing schools and jobs with minorities, and they have also seen what happens when people run. While the younger generation is still deeply troubled about race, there is a new willingness to interact socially and professionally with racial minorities in a way that three decades ago would have been unimaginable.

The minority group most likely to transform the racial complexion of Beltway is Hispanics (specifically Mexican Americans), not African Americans. Hispanics—Mexicans—are the new kids on the block. While Mexicans are not "white," the racial dynamics between whites and Mexicans have fundamentally different social, historical, political and economic contexts than the racial interplay between whites and African Americans.[20] Hispanics have not faced the same degree of segregation as African Americans, and this social reality has insulated Chicago's Hispanics from the extreme hardship facing those who are poor and black, making them less vulnerable to economic downturns and the effect of poverty and crime.[21] In the minds of many Beltway whites, there is a sense that of all the minority groups out there, Mexicans—who often act and seem more like the Irish, Poles, and Italians who came before them—are distinct from, or at least "preferable" to blacks.

The willingness of working-class white Chicagoans to share their neighborhood with second- and third-generation Mexicans does not alter the fact that racism between whites and blacks is deeply entrenched and still quite dangerous. There is no question that blacks remain the ultimate "out-group" racially. Blacks have come to symbolize urban decay and the ghetto in a way that Mexicans simply do not. While racial stereotypes lead whites to assume that all Mexicans are gangbangers, these preconceived notions pale in comparison to the racist assumptions and ideology reserved for African Americans. However, the fact that working-class whites have not fled at the first sight of nonwhite faces suggests the possibility for a limited amount of optimism for racial integration in the years to come.

CLASS CONSCIOUSNESS AND CONSUMPTION: WORKING-CLASS CULTURE AND MATERIALISM

In practical terms, Beltway's inhabitants are not quite middle-class. Educational attainment remains modest. Most people hold high school diplomas or maybe an associate degree, but not a four-year college degree.[22] Like most Americans, Beltway residents seem uncomfortable with class and resist class labels. While they might describe the area as "middle-class," they rarely describe themselves in the same clear-cut terms. Scholars, journalists, and policymakers might categorize Beltway as working- and lower-middle-class. Beltway's own Congressman Lipinski refers to his constituents as the "working middle class." Pollsters employ more scientific language such as "low to middle income, low education voters." Ex-Republican and Reform Party presidential candidate Patrick Buchanan, a self-styled neoconservative populist, employs more poetic language: "those who work with their hands, tools, and machines." The sociologist Herbert Gans uses the more general expression "Middle America" in response to Americans' tendency to refer to ourselves as middle-class regardless of our income level.[23] Most notably, one 40-year-old woman in Beltway evocatively captured the postindustrial notion of class by describing her neighbors and herself as "the children of factory workers."

Beltway's average household income places its residents right in the middle of the nation's income distribution (see Table 3).[24] But this begs the question: what precisely are Beltway residents in the middle of? Postindustrialism and late capitalism replace the industrial era fueled by steel, autos, and manufacturing. During the 1950s and 1960s, rising rates of home-ownership created a new affluence among working-class people, a phenomenon Christopher Lasch describes as the "embourgeoisment" of blue- and pink-collar Americans.[25] However, despite the attention paid to the jump in the number of millionaires during the dot-com revolution, income inequality has increased steadily since the 1970s. Incomes, adjusted for inflation, plunged in the early 1990s for all but the wealthiest 20 percent. Median family income—half of the nation's families earn less and half earn more—was slightly less than $49,000 in 1999. This is not to say working families are not doing better than they once were. Rising hours more than rising wages have pushed up family income. From 1995 to 1998, middle-income family members added more than 70 hours a year to their work time. In a recent *New York Times*

TABLE 3   FINANCIAL STATISTICS
OF BELTWAY RESIDENTS

	1960	1970	1980	1990	2000
Average years of education	10.2	11.5	11	N/A[a]	N/A
Average family income	7,584	12,467	25,176	39,523	N/A
Adjusted average family income[b]	44,214	49,120	45,065	41,016	N/A
Homeowning residents (%)	75	N/A	68	73	N/A

[a] 31% of Beltway residents received more than a high school education.
[b] Calculated in 1996 dollar values.

piece, Louis Uchitelle writes, "No one argues that middle income families cannot put food on the table, pay the mortgage, own a car or two, or take a modest vacation. What stresses them...are the outlays of middle-class life: new clothes, child care, lessons for the children, restaurants, movies, home decoration, computers, big-screen television sets, stereo systems, Christmas gifts, and saving for college and retirement."[26]

A generation ago the working classes believed, without a shadow of a doubt, that the lives of their children would be better than the previous generation's. Increasing uncertainty and the fear that future generations will face downward mobility now replace this more optimistic worldview. Sons and daughters of blue-collar aristocrats found themselves caught between a rock and a hard place. People with connections landed well-paying city jobs. Some working-class workers claimed the few living-wage union jobs that remained. And still others moved into the low-level white-collar "sweat shop" jobs of the new economy where employees face frequent lay-offs in the face of cyclical corporate cost-cutting and downsizing. This low-level service work in insurance or sales requires workers to keep long hours, provides minimal benefits without a union's bargaining power, and offers wages that hardly keep up with the cost of living. Most middle-income families subsidize the appearance of middle-class affluence by having two incomes. Since the 1960s, two incomes are no longer either a choice or a preference; they have become an economic fact of life. In the case of Beltway, Middle America's appearance of affluence is not quite what it seems. On the surface, the people of Beltway appear to live comfortably in fastidiously maintained bungalows. But at the end of the month, after the mortgage payments, credit card bills, and assorted household expenses, as one woman explains, "There's nothing left." While men may take pride in the fact "my wife doesn't have to work," many full-time homemakers take seasonal work in retail or find temporary jobs. These women are poised to take a job in case of a work-related injury or a lay-off. Many men, in good city jobs, scrounge to get as much overtime as their supervisors will allow. Many fathers find that weekends spent with family and friends are luxuries saved up for special occasions. Other men moonlight in one, maybe even two, extra jobs working security or freelancing as contractors. When an economic catastrophe such as divorce, unemployment, illness, or death strikes, families leading idyllic "lower-middle-class" existences may quickly be overcome by the harsh realities of downward mobility and American-style poverty. Most people have merely two or three missed mortgage payments between them and the collection agency.

While Beltway residents' economic futures may be less secure than their parents' generation, they do have more to consume than previous generations.[27] For in the wake of deindustrialization and the rise of the hi-tech and service sectors, the promise of getting ahead and having social mobility has been replaced by the magical illusion of consumption. These children and grandchildren of laborers who toiled in Chicago's factories and stockyards do not simply sell their labor; they produce a particular philosophy which animates the symbols and rituals of everyday life. In a very real sense, purchasing a house is the primary way the working- and lower-middle-class people of Beltway experience capitalism.

The brick bungalows on tiny patches of green fortify residents against a world filled with uncertainty. Living in Beltway means you can be a working man or woman during the day and a bourgeois property owner at night. A house offers a mark of achievement and a sense of stability. The investment in a home links a homeowner's future to the futures of his/her neighbors and a locality's surrounding institutions. A house embodies the material form of a lifetime of hard work and sacrifice. This house is "what I will leave my children." It is a "tombstone." It is a "part of me."

As the people of Beltway see it, the middle class is the moral class. Middle-class Americans are ordinary folks trying to live by traditional rules of working hard, saving for the future, and being loyal to family and country. The conservative social theorist Irving Kristol once wrote, "It is only the common people who remain loyal to the bourgeois ethos... the commonsense values of the working and lower middle class had an intimate and enduring relation to mundane realities that are relatively immune to speculative enthusiasm." Still Kristol noted, "The middle-class ideal of the common good, consisting mainly of personal security under the law, personal liberty under the law, and a steadily increasing material prosperity for those who apply themselves to that end[,] is not all that bad," and he concluded, "especially when compared to the pretensions of intellectuals."[28] The power of middle-class ideals among the lower middle class—and even the working class—has become one of the defining social and political ideologies in modern American life. Middle-class morality is synonymous with protecting traditional neighborhoods, family ideals, religious values, the work ethic, schools, love of country, and the security concerns of the lower middle class. The general feeling in America is that you are middle-class if you say so. Beltway residents, like many other Americans, define their claim to middle-class status in terms of not being poor and of earning enough to have some choice about where to live and how to live. To them, being middle-class means "attempting to claim a sense of personal responsibility by protecting themselves as best they can from the whims of employers, believing what one has achieved is due to one's hard work and efforts, and by owning as much of their home as possible."[29] Indeed, the residents of Beltway rely on the purchase of their house and the display of household objects to make the last garden come to life, and yet it is the consumption surrounding the house that masks the imperfections on the face of the American Dream. In this postindustrial, consumer age, the industrial-era notion of a working class defined by the relations of production seems ill equipped to capture the fragile, marginalized, and materialistic nature of life for working people in the United States today. "During the Depression, a workingman was judged by the ability to live within his means. Being sociable, not showing off, all these things proved one's moral worth."[30] At one time, the relations of production dictated the nature of working-class life. Today, working men and women find meaning beyond the plant or the workplace. We now live in an age where people are judged by what and how they consume; it is the relations of consumption that dictate the pattern of everyday life.

READING THE NEIGHBORHOOD LANDSCAPE: INTERPRETING THE LAST GARDEN

If you fly into Chicago on a premium airline such as United or American, you will land at O'Hare International Airport. O'Hare looks the way a major international airport is supposed to look, with tremendous marble concourses and vaulted glass ceilings. If, on the other hand, you happen to be traveling to Chicago on one of the "economy" carriers such as Southwest or ATA, you will most likely be landing at Midway Airport. As the plane begins its descent, it is hard to figure out where an airbus can land because the hundreds of square brick houses encircling the runways look as if they might engulf the airport. The closer you get to the ground, the more clearly you can make out the distinctive one-story bungalows sitting on postage stamp–sized lots. You might be surprised to see how many of the tiny backyards have been swallowed up by above-ground pools. Then, as the wheels are ready to hit the ground, it seems as if you might collide with someone's roof or a street light. As the plane pulls up to the gate, you might muse about the people living in the neat houses with tiny backyards so close to the airport's noise and pollution. A gray sound barrier wall is the only thing that separates the busy, cramped airport from all the people living in the brick bungalows.

Just to the north, perched on the city limits and bordered on one side by Midway Airport and on the other side by area factories and the railway yards, sits Beltway (see Map 4). The large number of soot-producing enterprises in the area gives the neighborhood a drab, gray veneer. Yet a lot of visitors are surprised to learn that it is still within the city limits. Beltway residents take pride in the fact that their neighborhood has a quiet "suburban" feel. The houses were all built around the same time by enterprising developers in the 1950s and '60s.

Beltwayites say they do not mind the sweet, pungent smell of corn syrup from the Purcell Plant or the fumes that linger in the air because of the planes landing and taking off at Midway; to Beltway's inhabitants such noxious odors are simply "the smell of work." While the factories, airport, and railway yards still serve as fortifications protecting Beltwayites from the rest of the city, the economic and demographic transformations of the past five decades have left their mark on Beltway's landscape. Beltway's industrial district is a graveyard of smokestacks, graffiti-covered abandoned buildings, and debris-filled vacant lots. Teenagers do not go to the warehouses looking for after-school jobs now; they vandalize the dilapidated buildings and use the old industrial district for illicit activities away from the intrusive gaze of adults. The empty factories and warehouses stand as monuments to the heyday of manufacturing and industry. On Beltway's outskirts sit flop houses and disreputable bars serving area transients and other local undesirables. Beltway's commercial district, once affectionately known as the "corner" to locals, has more empty storefronts than occupied ones.

The East Ward alderman, Jim Olivetti, has made a conscious effort to keep up appearances along the old business strip, so there are attractive flower planters, the streets are always swept, and graffiti are removed immediately. But even the labors of the city's Streets and Sanitation Department cannot hide the fact that the commercial district is dying. The airport authority purchased the Runway Diner and then demolished the building to create a green zone for the airport. Hart Hardware, Beltway's oldest business, closed its doors after 75 years because it

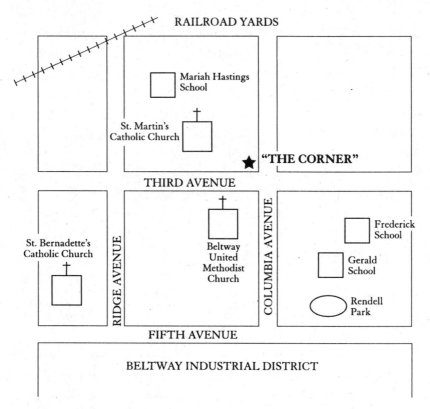

RAILROAD YARDS

Mariah Hastings School

St. Martin's Catholic Church

★ "THE CORNER"

THIRD AVENUE

St. Bernadette's Catholic Church

RIDGE AVENUE

Beltway United Methodist Church

COLUMBIA AVENUE

Frederick School

Gerald School

Rendell Park

FIFTH AVENUE

BELTWAY INDUSTRIAL DISTRICT

Map 4.   The Beltway neighborhood. This drawing is not to scale.

could not compete with the big suburban malls. Joe Demb shut down his barbershop after his failing health forced him to retire. The shop remained vacant for nearly a year before a flower wholesaler whose customers are street vendors hawking bouquets at intersections and highway off-ramps moved in to replace him.

Beltwayites' experiences in neighborhoods that have "gone down" have made them skilled diagnosticians when it comes to monitoring the condition of the urban landscape. They recognize these economic changes and the spread of desolate, forgotten spaces as the first symptoms of urban decay and disorder. The ghetto's chaos starts out as ne-

glected areas where residents have simply begun to "let things go a little." Over time, such neglect turns into abandonment, and so the blight
and chaos spread to lay waste to formerly good, safe, and decent places
to live.

In Beltwayites' view of the world, the spread of decay and disorder
has a racial and indeed racist subtext. Low-income minorities, specifically
poor blacks, are the carriers of the devastating effects of the ghetto's chaos.
Armchair anthropologists view the ghetto's landscape and the "patho-
logical" behavior of poor inner-city blacks as a social disease that destroys
economic stability and decency. A 70-year-old Beltway businessman and
homeowner's description of the ghetto provocatively captures the
horrified anxiety of working- and lower-middle-class Beltway residents.
"If you were to drive east all the way to Lake Michigan. Well, [let's just
say] they wasted the bomb on Hiroshima, they should've just set this
[poor, black] population down anywhere and they would've done the
same thing [as the bomb]. It looks like Hiroshima or burned out Berlin
and this is the problem." This lifelong Chicagoan declares, "This is a good
town, Chicago is a good town. And I can certainly understand the migration of the black man here looking to better himself.... So you can't
take the whole. But the bad has held down those good people." As Beltwayites read the landscape, they are quick to rely on knee-jerk racist explanations and interpretations about how these changes came to be. The
viewpoint of a city contractor living in Beltway invokes the familiar
racism of working-class whites. "The whole city is going down the toi-
let, that fucking Mayor Daley. If his father knew what he was doing, he'd
turn in his grave. Used to be that when you got a job, you got those jobs
for life and you could raise a family. Now taxes and all that shit are killing
the working man," he insists. "We're paying to support all the fucking
niggers and minorities in this city. I tell you, if this city keeps going the
way it's going, it's going to drive all the good working people right out.
I mean niggers don't pay taxes. Spics don't pay taxes. If we leave, there'll
be nothing left." The anger and vitriolic racism in this man's comments
are undeniable. Yet the naked racism of the comments should not dis-

tract us from the uncomfortable reality that his anger grows out of a correct assessment of working-class Americans' declining fortunes. For the average salaried worker, the real purchasing power of his or her wages has actually decreased in the past decade. Working-class whites may unjustly (and incorrectly) blame minorities for stagnating wages, but the most disturbing aspect of the contractor's statements is that these feelings of economic precariousness and working-class frustration grow out of economic truth. His statements teach us that in order for leaders and society at large to redress racism, we will need to take hold of the feelings of vulnerability that enflame such enmities.

It is also important to point out that such extreme expressions of racism are highly unusual in Beltway. Most of the time, racial animosities lie just beneath the surface to be invoked when the situation demands it to make sense of a particular event.[31] Beltway's homespun populists hold up the physical decay of the ghetto as irrefutable evidence of widespread social breakdown. The existence of the ghetto proves, beyond a shadow of a doubt, that the world is coming apart at the seams.

In the wake of civil rights and suburbanization, white activists and homeowners have indeed become more sophisticated about disentangling the concepts of race and class. Whites in Beltway claim that racial integration is possible, but they put the burden on the shoulders of the new arrivals. Minorities, Beltwayites believe, will be accepted as long as they work to keep up their homes and have incomes and occupations that are similar to their neighbors. Beltwayites believe, that all prospective garden dwellers must understand the importance of maintaining property and properly caring for and supervising children. Maintaining your home is a courtesy extended to neighbors whose property values are contingent on the condition of houses on the rest of the block. Children reflect back on the morality, decency, and conduct of their parents. Kids running the streets and causing trouble become a burden and a potential threat to the community at-large.

White Beltwayites say they will share their neighborhood with a carefully selected group of minorities, because white homeowners have seen what happens when panicked whites flee at the first sign of racial turnover. In the words of a 35-year Beltway resident who is a veteran of the battles over segregation and housing, "Now I say when you see a minority move in, you say 'hi' to 'em. Some of them are better than the whites we've got here now." Indeed, Beltway's small, but growing, population of Hispanics (less than 8 percent in 1990, but 20 percent by 2000) has higher average levels of education and income than their white counterparts. Under such conditions, Beltwayites declare, "I don't care who moves in, as long as they take good care of things."

GANGS AND GRAFFITI

The deindustrialized landscape is only one challenge confronting Beltway residents; despite idyllic pronouncements about the civility of their neighborhood, Beltwayites regularly push up against dangerous urban problems such as gangs and violence. Young people in every part of Chicago, as across the nation, hang out on corners, get into fights, deal drugs, and resort to deadly violence. While families in Beltway feel safe and secure because the lower-middle-class environment in which they live offers residents a certain amount of distance from the dangers of the streets, only the most naïve Beltwayites believe that living two or three miles away from high crime neighborhoods (areas of the city known as Murder Alley) insulates them completely from violence. The same social and economic forces that have created open-air drug markets and drive-by shootings in ghetto neighborhoods have eaten away at the economic security and stability of more affluent communities. It is just that the demographic characteristics of communities like Beltway, coupled with access to more resource-rich systems of formal social control (such as the police department and courts), drive local criminal activity underground. In Beltway, you must look beyond tidy lawns and houses to see the more troubling aspects of life in the garden.

In Chicago, gang members use five- and six-point stars, gothic lettering, and distinctive colors and codes to carve out a gang's sphere of influence, declare wars, and warn trespassers of the dangers of wandering into rival territory.[32] Two or three gangs operate in the Beltway neighborhood at any given time. Gangs and gang membership tend to be as fluid and loose as the social peer groups of young people in which gangs take root. In the mid-1990s, local law enforcement officials disagreed about the number of active gang members in the Beltway area. In 1996, estimates ranged from 40 to 100; it is often difficult to distinguish between hard-core members and more peripheral "wannabes."

Gangs have been a fact of life in Chicago since the early part of the twentieth century, and the majority of these early gang members were white. Despite the fact that the sons of European immigrants invented gangs in the United States, it is "supergangs" or corporate gangs like the Gangster Disciples and Latin Kings that regularly grab newspaper headlines today. Contemporary urban gangs have their strongest presence in high-poverty areas of the city, where the majority of their members are racial and ethnic minorities. The sociologist Sudhir Venkatesh states that gangs operating in the ghetto communities he studies have a highly visible and surprisingly integrated role in the day-to-day lives of gang members and nongang residents alike. A social vacuum created by the absence of legitimate economic enterprises and institutions allows gangs to perform central economic, social, and institutional roles. In striking contrast, Beltway's local gang problem is more opaque. Beltway's gang members do not engage in open-air drug dealing and rarely resort to deadly violence. Indeed, most of Beltway's adult population remains blissfully unaware of the level of local gang activity.[33] Neighbors assume that gang members are outsiders who periodically invade the neighborhood or that families living in the apartments along Third and Fifth Avenues "brought the troublemakers" into Beltway.

However, when a gang member was shot by a member of a rival gang in Rendell Park, Ford Village residents in the eastern section of Beltway became aware of the danger posed by area gang members. Dozens of anxious neighbors attended meetings organized by the park advisory board and Gerald School parents. Local law enforcement officials downplayed the incident. One police officer remarked that the victim was only wounded in the leg "even though he was shot at point-blank range." The officer tried to assuage local residents' fears with the information that the shooter had never intended to kill his victim. Other residents talked about how the victim "was no saint" and had had several run-ins with the police himself. Chicago police officers accustomed to the deadly gang violence of ghetto neighborhoods described the incident as minor and laughable in comparison to the activities of the hardcore gang-bangers operating in other sections of the city. Race colored these discussions, as residents and police could not imagine white kids living in comfortable (that is, not poor) surroundings engaging in deadly gang violence. The police and parents dismissed these local gang members as white kids acting out their own playground version of the thug life inspired by music videos and song lyrics. Police officers living in Beltway believed that they could handle these kids, who were hanging out in the schoolyards and talking back to the cops when they were asked to move along. "There are fights, but I got into fights as a kid." "Gangs are a problem in the projects." White kids who go to Catholic school and who live with both their parents do not fit the typical profile of a gang member. Neighbors assured themselves that the local gangbangers like the Popes and Disciples were just parodies of the real thing.

The Rendell Park shooting hardly touched those living in the more affluent western section of Beltway. Beltway Civic League activists heard about the incident but viewed the matter as something for the people at the park and the school to handle. Some Beltwayites in the western section of the neighborhood blamed the violence on the "white trash" element or the "hillbillies" living in the rental housing in Ford Village. Others offered a more sociological explanation. They said these gang members came from the small settlement of Appalachian families living in the eastern section of the neighborhood. Such youngsters, they argued, were prone to violence because of the violent gun culture of rural Tennessee and West Virginia. At the time of the Rendell Park shooting, most of Beltway's adult residents—in east and west Beltway—clung to the conviction that the ordered appearance of their homes, the white complexions of the vast majority of their neighbors, and the neighborhood's working-class respectability inoculated Beltway from the threat of deadly gang violence.

A small group of voices, however, could be heard speaking out with concern about Beltway's young people and the area's homegrown gangs. Joe Trenton, a community organizer who witnessed the process of neighborhood turnover within the Bungalow Belt's eastern section, insists that the appearance of graffiti is the first harbinger that a neighborhood is going to be overrun by gangs. According to Trenton, crime is the biggest threat posed to neighborhoods like Beltway. In stable working-class communities, crime may not be as "apparent as other parts of the city," but "gang crime is crawling into these neighborhoods so slowly that it is insidious. It starts with graffiti, then kids hanging out, then the kids move into some abandoned building." An elementary school guidance counselor in one of Beltway's schools recalls trying to organize a meeting for parents about the gangs and how to recognize the warning signs of a youngster's gang activity. "Nobody came, they just didn't think it was a problem here." A mother of a teenage daughter who was skipping school and socializing with members of the Popes gang warned that "disaffected teens and the graffiti fight are the most serious problems facing this community." This same mother said her neighbors had "buried their head in the sands" to the dangers gangs like the Popes, Satan's Disciples, and Two-Sixers posed to Beltway.

◆　　◆　　◆

Working-class people residing in places like Beltway see America as a three-tiered society made up of the welfare class, a middle class, and an increasingly affluent upper class. Beltway residents do not like to be reminded about their "in-between" status with the Haves on one side and the Have-Nots on the other. In-between status terrifies the garden's inhabitants. Consumption, ritualistic displays of housepride, and a fanatical concern for order serve as talismans to keep socioeconomic insecu-

rities at bay. The social, economic, and political truths that breed economic inequality remain invisible to the people of Beltway. Instead, low-
income blacks trapped in the ghetto become the unwitting scapegoats
for poverty, filth, and decay. Even though the rich and powerful are no
better, economically disadvantaged minorities' societal stigma (as well
as their close physical and social proximity to working-class whites)
makes them easier targets for garden dwellers' inflammatory politics of
resentment.

Writing about the ethnic whites who fought to improve conditions
in the slum neighborhoods surrounding the stockyards, the famous
community organizer Saul Alinsky states that in the early days of the
Back of the Yard residents' activism, the group's largely Polish-American membership fought discrimination against themselves by denounc-
ing all forms of injustice. "Through the years group members mounted
victory upon victory and moved steadily up the ladder from the position
of Have-Nots to that of Have-a-Little-and-Want-Mores. In the end, it
seemed as though these working-class whites willingly traded in their
revolutionary dreams for a mess of property, power, and the grand illusion of security." In Alinsky's words, "the dreams of achievement that
make men fight were replaced by restless nightmares of fear: fear of
change, fear of losing material possessions." Today the descendants of
European immigrant laborers are a part of the city's establishment.
Rather than fighting for change, they are working desperately to keep
their neighborhoods unchanged. Alinsky concludes that working-class
white homeowners "are not trying to keeps blacks out, but rather trying to keep their people in."[34] For residents swept up in white flight, the
experience of fleeing has made them feel victimized by the Civil Rights
era and fuels their profound attachment to the area. Beltway resident
and activist Lydia Donovan explains: "What you have to understand is
that for many people they have had to move once or twice so what they
say is based on their experience. Like when Martin Luther King
marched on Chicago, he went to places like Marquette Park and so on.
So, many people who live here have had to move once or twice. For

them, Beltway is the last stand." The younger generation knows what can happen when the bad neighbors start to outnumber the good ones, so they too are invested in keeping the destructive forces of decay, disorder, and crime at a distance. But this younger generation is more sophisticated about race, and more and more of them say they are willing to share the last garden with nonwhites as long as the newcomers accept the locals' distinctive sense of place. In essence, class now overshadows race in terms of what residents want to protect within the Beltway community. However, in Beltway, adults rarely treated the presence of local, white gang-members as a real community problem. Popular wisdom and common sense assured parents and grandparents that gangs grow out of the poverty and disorder of the ghetto. Kids living in nice brick bungalows with both of their parents ought to be safe from the dangers of the street. In the chapter that follows, we see how Beltwayites' zealous devotion to the garden's ordered and idyllic appearance prevented residents from seeing that the greatest threat to their precious way of life lurked among their own children.

TWO

A Precious Corner of the World

BLOCK PARTIES AND IDYLLIC POSSIBILITIES

Joyce Czawjowski breathes a sigh of relief; for once the weather reports will be right, "the weather is just perfect," she assures herself. Eighties with a just a touch of humidity in the air, not the usual blistering summer heat Chicagoans have come to expect in a city that was once prairie for as far as the eye could see. It will be a wonderful day for the Midvale Street annual block party, an event Joyce and her neighbors have been busy planning for months.

In the front yard, Joyce's husband Lou, a solid wall of a man who works as a Chicago firefighter, is completely engrossed in the task of caring for his lawn. Lou hoses down the walkway to the bungalow with the care one would take to vacuum the corners of a priceless rug. The bleached white concrete is so clean that all day long the Czawjowskis' considerate guests will be careful not to drop food on the path for fear it would leave a stain. Lou surveys the lawn that looks so good you want to touch the grass to make sure it is real.

At almost every house on the block men, women, and children busy themselves with preparations. Picnic tables and lawn chairs are moved from their customary locations out back to the perfect square patches of lawn out front. The first guests arrive in the early afternoon, and Lou tells the kids to go out back to the pool to cool off. Within minutes, three youngsters have stripped down to bathing suits. The voices of annoyed adults barking orders like "no water fights" and "no more cannonballs" punctuate the sounds of water splashing and children squealing with delight. Each parent will take a shift supervising the pool area.

Face-painting, a giant Jumping Jack (one of those giant trampolines with padded walls), raffles, and games are just a few of the activities planned for the day. Some of the younger children cannot wait to see the horses from the police department's mounted unit. One child asks her mother if she can feed the horses some carrots she has dug out of the family refrigerator. Older kids like Lou and Joyce's 13-year-old daughter Courtney and her friend Lisa crinkle their noses at the idea of doing such "little kid stuff." But by the early afternoon, the two 13-year-olds sport matching butterfly tattoos, courtesy of the face-painting lady. In the afternoon, a man dressed in a threadbare, stuffed animal costume suddenly appears and starts to hand out toys from the Dollar Store to the children. There is a brief debate among the parents about what the costume is supposed to be; some think a dog, others a rabbit or maybe a bear. The man in the costume is actually Anthony Frank, the block's precinct captain. The toys and Tony come courtesy of West Ward Alderman Stan Romanoski.

Lou says he is excited to sample the Mexican-style skirt steak that his next-door neighbor Letty Ortega's mother prepares every year. Next year, Lou promises his guests, he will learn to make skirt steak for himself. Such all-day barbecue extravaganzas merge lunch and dinner together into one unbutton-your-pants meal. A guest jokes how she stopped eating last night in anticipation of all the food she would eat today. Lou's fellow firefighter Jesse Johnson and Jesse's wife Serena have just arrived. They are among the few people at the party who do not live in the neighborhood. The Johnsons confide to some partygoers that this is the first time they been to the western section of the Bungalow Belt. The Johnsons are African American.

Dan, one of Lou and Joyce's neighbors, calls a couple of his boys to help him carry the cones and wooden saw-horses out back from his garage. It is time for the disc jockey to set up, and the block party committee has permission to close off the street. Almost everyone on the block will join in the revelry. Dancing and music will continue until past midnight. How can you resist joining in when 40 or 50 of your neighbors are doing the Macarena or the Electric Slide? The block party committee brings out a cake to surprise the Majerskis for their fortieth wedding anniversary. Mr. and Mrs. Majerski have lived on this block for most of that time. The DJ invites the pair to take the first dance of the evening. Everyone applauds as the couple twirls about on the grass to an old Sinatra tune.

A SENSE OF PLACE ON THE LEVEL OF NEIGHBORHOOD

For the remainder of the year, neighbors may complain and gossip, but block parties provide almost perfect moments for residents to put aside their differences to eat, drink, and dance in the streets. Everyone basks in the unique quality that makes the neighborhood worth defending. How people think and feel about places—the sense of place—is a phrase employed by geographers to emphasize that places are significant because they are the focus of personal feelings. "Certain localities," writes the historian John Brickenhoff Jackson, "have an attraction which gives us a certain indefinable sense of well-being. Indeed the meanings given to a place may be so strong that they become a central part of the people experiencing them."[1]

As the last garden spot in Chicago, Beltway roots its distinctive sense of place in the metaphor of a garden as a place of cultivated order and abundance. The sense of place thus serves as a potent catalyst for civic

activism in response to even the most minor violations of the visual landscape. To solicitous homeowners, small violations in the garden's ordered
appearance (incivilities such as graffiti, trash on the street, unkempt
lawns, and potholes) represent symbolic assaults on the safety and security the people of Beltway have labored to create. Without question,
order is one of the fundamental goals of the social world; it is necessary
for social actors to act, and is integral to a sense of balance and equilib-
rium. In this sense, while the garden symbolizes order and abundance,
then the ghetto represents its opposites: chaos and decay.

The growing mobility and transience of these times make old notions
of places as settled and coherent more difficult to sustain.[2] "This very
feeling that we live in an unstable and uncertain world makes us long
for a secure and stable place all the more. To be rooted in a place is to
have a secure point from which to look out on the world, a firm grasp
of one's position in the order of things, and a significant spiritual and
psychological attachment to somewhere in particular. The material use
of a place cannot be separated from the psychological use; the daily round
that makes day-to-day life possible comes to take on profound emotional
meaning through the very capacity to fulfill specific goals. Such material and psychic rewards thus combine to create the feeling of shared
community. Location establishes a special collective interest among individuals."[3] The willingness of local residents to intervene for the common good depends on conditions of mutual trust and solidarity among
neighbors, a phenomenon Robert Sampson, Stephen Raudenbush, and
Felton Earls term "collective efficacy."[4] In a sense, the neighborhood is
a "vested interest spilling out of the individual household and project-
ing itself onto neighbors, streets, local businesses, schools, and other institutions."[5]In the words of Morris Janowitz and Gerald Suttles, "The
local neighborhood becomes a catchment area in which accountability
is identified and made collective; a bounded group in which responsibility is joint yet so narrowly circumscribed that its members can real-
istically contribute to the task of self-regulation, the collective interests
in the futures of children and the caretaking of the nearby physical en-

vironment bring to life the community's moral, social, and political functions. Much if not all the physical plant of human society is sessile; that is, most of our public possessions must be located where they can be guarded, cared for, kept clean, or at least unharmed. Residents who live near these public resources become the public custodians who look out for school windows, the disposal of waste, and the informal surveillance of street life."[6]

Sociologist Sharon Zukin states that the term "landscape" can be used as a tool for cultural analysis for it connotes "a contentious, compromised product of society...a point of view."[7] Beltwayites' devotion to the garden and their belief in its unique sense of place dramatize the "point of view" of its working-class inhabitants. Former Alderman John Puchinski's description of Beltway brings to life the connections between the landscape and the values of Beltway neighbors: "The Beltway community is really a stereotype of the whole ward here. It's very white, ethnic, a serving community. A lot of blue-collar workers, a lot of people who have worked hard to buy their home, who have worked hard to put their kids through school.... It's a very conservative, roll-up-the-sleeves type of community. They work hard, and not so many people were born with silver spoons. Most of the people worked hard for what they have and I think that has a lot to do with how people take pride in their property, take pride in their schools, just have that work ethic, that pride in the neighborhood."[8] "The neighborhood has a good family life," insists Franny Wertelka, a lifelong Southwest Sider and professional community organizer. Beltway "is almost hidden from the rest of the city. If I said to someone on the North Side, 'Have you heard of Beltway? they'd probably say, 'What?' Now I don't think Beltway has that kind of attraction for gentrifiers on the North Side, it has a different kind of appeal. This place has an old-fashioned kind of solidity. The old-timers remain involved and that catches the attention of the baby boomers because now they are getting involved in things like the Neighborhood Watch. It's a very solid, concrete neighborhood." According to Lillian Crimmins, "The best neighbors I've ever had in my life have been in the city. In the Southwest Side, you're loyal to the White Sox, you're loyal to the Bears. You're loyal to the values of the neighborhood and you don't question it. People just think this is the greatest place."

A BASTION OF NEIGHBORHOOD STABILITY

Beltwayites are tied together through a dense network of acquaintanceship, extended families, residential stability, common ethnic, racial, and class backgrounds, vibrant community organizations, and powerful institutional ties. For the most part, Beltwayites know their neighbors. Residents often comment on the "small-town" feel of the neighborhood. Lydia Donovan explains, "Beltway is diverse but not chaotic. The population isn't on top of you. It's not high density and still residential. Well, people in a lot of ways are isolated out here and part of that they want and like." Residents take great pride in the ordered appearance of the neighborhood. Cleanliness is one of the first things neighbors mention when describing why they believe Beltway is a special place. According to 38-year-old Neely Martin, the mother of two who works for the park district, "Beltway, you're in Chicago. It's nice. People are friendly. You feel comfortable." To 35-year-old homemaker and teacher's aide Joyce Czawjowski, "We like Beltway for the most part. It's clean. We have good public transportation. I like the city life where the houses are close together and you can open your window and yell at your neighbor. I like that. That's what I'm used to." Congressman Lipinski, a lifelong Southwest Sider, started out as a city employee, working his way up through the ranks of rough-and-tumble Chicago machine politics to be elected congressman in the 1970s. He describes Beltway as "a homogeneous community" where people "have always been very much involved in parish affairs, Little League, and once upon a time, Civic Leagues." Lipinski continues, "It's a very patriotic community. But the most outstanding feature is how clean it is. As a city neighborhood, it is often said that one could not only eat off the streets, but eat off the alleys."

Neighbors like to say "Everybody here knows what everybody else is doing, everybody looks out for everybody else." Toni Capelevski, a 40-year-old wife of a Chicago police officer and mother of two middle school–age daughters attending Hastings School recalls that when she first moved to the neighborhood she was struck "by how friendly people were. In two days I had met half the people on my block. They knocked on my door and now I think I have keys to almost everybody's houses and stuff like that. So I found people very friendly and neighborly." Although family networks are not as dense as they once were in the old immigrant enclaves, there is a close-knit feel to the area, and families still pass down houses from generation to generation. A lifelong Beltway resident in her forties who is married to a Chicago firefighter, Crystal Kaiser says: "Everybody's nosey around here. Like last week there was a fire truck out on the block, it turns out my neighbor's carbon monoxide detector had gone off." According to Crystal, "it seemed as if the entire block had come out to see if they could help or, at the very least, hear about what had happened." If something "is happening on the block everybody's out. If I think something is going on, [of course] I'll go out and stand on my step to see what is going on."

Over coffee in her house, while we watch her two young daughters play, city worker, mother, and wife Neely Martin says feeling comfortable and being surrounded by people like herself makes Beltway more appealing than the suburbs. "I have friends in the suburbs and they have neighbors from California and they have Indians on one side of them who don't talk to them and they give 'em dirty looks. And it's not that other people are bad. It's just that a lot of people don't understand each other. Or they have really rich people next door, he's a doctor and she's a lawyer and they just moved in and you know they are only going to probably be there a year or two because they're going to be moving on." She explains, "You see, most of the people here I feel like I can relate to. Most of the people here have been in Chicago all their lives and the mother lives on one block and the sister lives on another. Like I went to high school with one of my neighbors and the other one has an uncle that works at the park district like me. I feel comfortable." When the owner of a beauty parlor by the name of Kathy Fenton lived in the suburbs with her twin sons and husband, she says, "I didn't know my neighbors down the street and my kids went to Catholic school and I didn't know half the people there." For Kathy, the difference between the garden and the suburbs is that "in the suburbs people are more to themselves…fast-paced, on the go, there was no familiarity with people. Here, things are closer; you're in walking distance to everything. I think it's a more close-knit community and people are more involved with their children." Toni Capelevski, who organizes the monthly bunco games, says she was drawn to the neighborhood because "we knew city workers lived here" and Beltway "is like a safety zone. We felt it was going to be people in our same situation. Our same type of lifestyle, maybe same educational background, same family values, this was the place for us. If we moved further south, we didn't know what we'd be dealing with. Here we felt like we'd fit in."

The ghetto that surrounds the garden serves as a constant reminder of the vulnerability of place and crime and disorder. What residents fear most is that the ghetto will devour the garden. Lara Owens, a 15-year Beltway resident who works as a police radio dispatcher and shares her bungalow with her boyfriend and a good-natured pug named Spike, says, "When I hear my mom talk about the neighborhoods she used to live in and how these areas are just the worst areas now.…I guess change is a part of everybody's life but if it's for the worse, you would think about how good it was and how much you had, and now you're afraid to go outside. Your friends would start to scatter and we'd all start selling our houses." Lara Owens's friend and neighbor Connie Patton chimes in, "My kids feel like they belong here, but I would move if this area got infested with gangs like a ghetto area."

Ultimately, the people of Beltway believe that neighbors working together "to take care of things and look out for one another" will ward off the ghetto's chaos. Whites' seemingly primordial fears about the arrival of nonwhites grow out of the conviction that the categories of minority and poor mean the same thing, and that lower-class whites and minorities cannot possibly share the garden inhabitants' values about proprietorship and guardianship for the community. "It's not blacks per se, it the kind of blacks that would move in," concerned homeowners insist. Mary Patillo-McCoy, in her account of life for lower-middle-class blacks living in Chicago's Groveland neighborhood, observes that black homeowners' fears concerning renters echo the concerns of working-class whites in Beltway. When middle-class blacks are faced with sharing their neighborhoods with lower-class blacks, they fear that poor blacks who rent rather than own their homes may not share the same values as their more affluent, homeowner neighbors. Obviously middle-class blacks do not say they are anxious about poor blacks because of race; however, they do express concerns about their neighbors on the basis of class and perceptions of class-based differences in values.[9] For the people of Beltway, working-class homeowners' racism takes shape in their endeavors to guard the physical plant of the community's resources.

DEFENDING BELTWAY

Beltway residents underlined their defensiveness about control of their residential areas when the Daley administration proposed the construction of affordable housing at the edge of Beltway in 1996. The city's rationale for proceeding with the plan grew out of new conventional wisdom that explains low-income housing's failure by pointing to the ill-conceived high-rise, high-density project template. Erecting massive housing complexes for poor people in communities already overwhelmed by high concentrations of poverty had proven an unmitigated failure. To urban planners and policymakers, the solution involves dispersing low-income residents throughout the city in stable neighborhoods. A second portion of the mayor's housing initiatives includes the

City Mortgage Program: a plan to subsidize mortgages through low-interest loans and federally funded grants to low-income first-time homebuyers. The plan's purpose is transform "renter" city dwellers into property tax–paying ones. A second less explicit goal of the plan is to break down Chicago's racial segregation by moving economically disadvantaged African Americans into places like Beltway. Both plans were greeted with widespread opposition from local activists and residents in Beltway. As one resident privately acknowledged, "Building a [project] in Beltway gives officials the best possible neighborhood at the lowest possible cost." Local residents cynically note that such a housing project would never be constructed in upscale Lincoln Park or Michigan Avenue's stylish "Magnificent Mile."

During one particularly heated Civic League meeting in April 1996, West Ward Alderman Romanoski was attacked by residents over the scatter zoning issue. The BCL invited the alderman to address the group at their monthly meeting. Even though he had spent the previous several weeks arguing not to have low-income housing built in Beltway, the audience of 30 residents—mostly retirees who had lived in the neighborhood upwards of 30 years—was in a rancorous frame of mind and itching for someone to blame. Indeed, the fact that the alderman vociferously opposed the scatter zoning plan was barely acknowledged; instead the newly elected Romanoski made a convenient punching bag.

A few weeks earlier, Civic League officers sent an angry letter to Mayor Daley's office declaring their opposition to "City Mortgage," a term Beltway residents spat out with contempt because they saw it as a thinly veiled euphemism for blockbusting. Beltway Civic League leaders argued the City Mortgage would enable people "who were not ready" for the responsibilities of home-ownership to purchase homes they could not afford. These homeowners would destabilize neighborhoods when they were forced to sell after a foreclosure. Or worse, they might stay in the neighborhood and be unable to maintain their property up to the standards the people of Beltway expected, thus driving down housing values for their neighbors. The city housing commissioner's response to the Civic

League letter was another letter filled with reassuring phrases and conciliatory language about "stabilizing neighborhoods" and "creating good neighbors." The letter ends with the commissioner assuring Civic League members that "strict requirements for the program would be enforced."

As Ron Zalinsky read the letter out loud to the crowd, neighbors rolled their eyes and howled in disbelief. Ron became a minister calling for responses from his loyal congregation. "Who is going to pay for this?" he bellowed. "Us, the taxpayers, and with interest," he boomed. People roared their angry approval. Stan Marino (a bellicose retiree who is revered as neighborhood folk hero for his frequent battles with the railroads over the traffic delays caused by train crossings) scoffed, "When they say they want to stabilize our community with this program...I say this community is already stabilized." Stan went on to suggest that the program was little more than a thinly veiled conspiracy sponsored by "churches, realtors, and synagogues" to drive down neighborhood housing prices. Jock Lyle, another retiree who remembers Englewood "when things got bad," called on his neighbors "to write letters to the City Council to remind them about what happened when [neighborhoods went down] before. Now even the projects got better when they got picky about who was living there." When Alderman Romanoski, the guest of honor, walked to the front of the church hall to address the crowd, it seemed that he might never have the chance to speak. Romanoski and his East Ward counterpart, Jim Olivetti, had declared their opposition to the plan; indeed the two men were scheduled to testify before the City Council Budget Committee hearings in the coming week. However, when the newly elected alderman informed the crowd that the decision was "out of my hands" since the city's powerful mayor and his equally powerful political machine backed the plan, the crowd of senior citizens looked as if they might leap out of their chairs and physically assault Romanoski. The audience interpreted the alderman's pessimistic view of their chances for blocking the legislation as a sort of betrayal. As the crowd hurled abuse at him, practically accusing him of being a collaborator with the enemy, Romanoski dropped the customarily self-conscious, guarded language of a politician to defend his commitment to their cause. His voice trembling with emotion, he declared, "I have opposed scatter zoning and City Mortgage. Why do these programs come to the West Ward where people have raised their families? There seems to be two sets of standards. Now I have been accused of being a racist on television [because of my stand on this issue]. I've been accused of keeping the West Ward lily-white. Why is this area always being singled out?"

A year later when local leaders once again attempted to broach the volatile topic of affordable housing—this time in the form of the proposed site for scatter zoning (to Beltwayites another euphemism for Section 8 and housing projects)—church leaders and sympathetic residents created the "The Welcoming Communities Task Force" in an effort to mediate between the city's housing commissioner and local residents. The task force planned to hold a series of town meetings throughout the community to discuss the issue and alleviate neighbors' fears. The first meeting would be held at the Good Shepherd Presbyterian Church. This time, Beltway Civic League officers joined forces with the neighboring Carver Heights Civic League to write a statement to be read at the first meeting. One longtime resident who was supportive of the Welcoming Committee's efforts described the letter as the most dangerous sort of race baiting. Others in the neighborhood viewed the letter as a simple statement of fact: the people of Beltway would not stand idly by and be forced to share their precious garden with people who had no respect for the sacrifice and work required in maintaining this precious corner of the world. The letter said:

> There are few, if any neighborhoods, that share the low crime, high value, and well-groomed appearance of the West Ward. The residents of the ward equally share the rewards of our hard work and efforts in our beautiful streets and alleys, gardens, parks, and schoolyards.
>
> To allow strangers to participate in these rewards due to the misguided efforts of our government truly is a slap in the face to those who have achieved their own dreams by hard work. Why should we, the current residents, be penalized for our hard work? You are penalizing us by diluting the end product of our work. You

are attempting to place people in our neighborhood who cannot afford, on their own, to live there.... Nobody helped my family and nobody helped my neighbors.

"Refugees from neighborhoods that have changed"—to use the code word for becoming black—"keep reliving their past experiences and continually search for signs that history might repeat itself. Indeed, it is difficult for veterans of neighborhood change to imagine a future that could be different from the past."[10] Maintaining Beltway as a bastion of neighborhood stability has become a sort of obsession requiring preemptive strikes and the vigilant guard of all good and decent neighbors. Watching old neighborhoods get absorbed into the ghetto devastated working-class whites. Memories of childhood and old routines were spat upon when the "lazy, undeserving, and dirty" people came. "How can ghetto dwellers have so little respect for themselves?" the people of Beltway wondered. "How can they live in such squalor?" Garden dwellers found it difficult to make sense of neighborhoods changing. Proximity to the ghetto keeps old wounds open and fresh. Cherished memories of lost places become chronic aches reminding people in places like Beltway of how close they have been to losing their place in the world. Among the younger generation, racial turnover is terrifying because class turnover represents such a serious threat to housing values. If the wrong kind of people move in, then property values plummet and crime rates skyrocket. "The issue isn't the color of their faces, it's the kind of people who move in."

THE BELTWAY CIVIC LEAGUE: TALES OF NEIGHBORHOOD PROPRIETORSHIP

Political scientist Robert Putnam laments the decline of civic life in the United States. "By almost every measure, America's direct engagement in politics and government has steadily and sharply fallen over the last generation."[11] Yet in the seemingly inhospitable environment of Midway Airport, factories, and the railway yards, Beltway defies Putnam's dire predictions. The people of Beltway maintain a tight-knit community characterized by what Putnam calls civic engagement.

Beltway "is an urban version of the 'little republic' Thomas Jefferson envisioned as one of democracy's local outposts. In the wake of suburbanization—as communities become increasingly rootless and atomized—" the people of Beltway struggle to maintain their distinctive way of life. Places like Beltway "have become endangered species. Amid what has become a nation of strangers,"[12] the people of Beltway honor the neighborhood, maintaining it with the same care they lavish on their cars and homes. Much of residents' activism takes root in their determination to "defend" Beltway from neighborhood change. According to Kathy Fenton, "Beltway is not going to go because you're gonna have people that are concerned. We have good citizens here. There are people that are aware of what's going on and if there was a crime wave, you would have neighbors bonding together." She continues, "I've gone door to door in this area for my work in the neighborhood and people may not always come out but they care and they will show it when it comes down to it. That's the biggest thing I've seen. . . . They're not afraid to stand together."

Area residents share a long history of civic activism. A zoning issue led to the founding of the Beltway Civic League during the spring of 1960. Local women staged a demonstration to prevent the expansion of a chemical factory into a densely populated residential section of the neighborhood. Nearly 150 women with young children in tow descended on City Hall carrying signs saying "Are We To Be Sacrificed?" and "A Tisket, A Tasket We Don't Want Our Kids in a Casket." One woman told a reporter from the *Chicago Sun-Times,* "We're here because families in the area put their life savings into their homes." The protest came to a swift conclusion when the demonstrators gave their alderman a petition with the signatures of 700 constituents who opposed the factory's proposal. The alderman worked quickly and denied the plant's request. Through this act, the people of Beltway had their first sweet taste of the power of collective action. In the wake of the victory on the rezoning project, area residents came together to form the Civic League. Over the past 35 years the Beltway Civic League leadership has worked on a wide variety of subjects affecting neighborhood life, ranging from zoning, pollution, incinerators, and public transportation to taxes, bussing, low-income housing, schools, and crime.

Ron Zalinsky, the longtime Beltway Civic League president, boasts that the group "is a watchdog" for the neighborhood. "We get input from people, we find out what people want and the organization is like a computer because we do the output." His friend Fred chimes in, "All the push is for the North and Northwest Sides of the city. The city forgets about us, and out of necessity we've become loud. We have to make noise. We have to make noise, without hollering or screaming we wouldn't get nothing. We're so far out and out of sight is out of mind." Ava Conrad, a one-time aldermanic candidate and local businesswoman, explains, "There is a lot of conservative activism. People are involved and just concerned with the community. The Beltway Civic League, they grab on to an issue and they just work on it." Arthur Straub, the owner and operator of a machine shop in the neighborhood, says, "The Beltway Civic League has covered many subjects and issues. I mean we've been out there on things that have dramatically impacted the entire city. We've been involved in a lot of issues and usually what happens is we have someone who sits down and digs up the facts. We always have plenty of emotion."

To Civic League members and other local activists, Beltway is a possession. This feeling of ownership is not metaphorical; residents believe they may claim the rights of ownership because of their status as homeowners and through the taxes they pay. To garden dwellers, the act of purchasing a house is analogous to buying stock in a corporation. As stockholders with controlling interests in the neighborhood, so to speak, they have a right and an obligation to involve themselves in every aspect of neighborhood life. This proprietorship of the neighborhood moves activists to focus on issues related to the visual landscape. The most obvious way of determining if an object is well maintained is through its appearance. Beltwayites believe that the manner in which an individual cares for possessions becomes a reflection back on the individual; neglect implies irresponsibility and carelessness. In the respectable, working- and lower-middle-class world the people of Beltway inhabit, sins against the ordered visual landscape and the sanctity of property are unforgiv- able. Failure to "keep up appearances" suggests that residents do not de- serve the privilege of being part of a precious, valued neighborhood. When one neighbor falls short and fails to uphold the community stan- dards, this failure reflects badly on the entire neighborhood. Because the people of Beltway derive a sense of pride and sense of themselves from where they live, residents' perceptions about the visual landscape are central to their everyday conceptions of themselves and the rest of the world. In this context, seemingly minor violations of the visual land- scape and efforts to keep the neighborhood clean by removing graffiti and demolishing abandoned buildings become powerful impetuses for collective action.[13]

Local residents' 15-year battle for a new library building is just one instance of the feeling of proprietorship and the strong emotional com- mitment that fuels this connection to *place*. A core group of neighbor- hood activists came together to pressure the city into replacing Beltway's small library storefront with a new state-of-the-art building. In 1979, future Illinois Governor Jim Edgar was in charge of new construction for the city's library system. When Edgar was scheduled to speak at an outdoor event in the city, Arthur Straub, Lydia Donovan, and some other Civic League members decided to use the speech as a launching pad for their library building campaign. Jim Hennessey, a retiree and another Civic League member, attached a six-foot-tall sign decorated with balloons to the back of his truck and found a parking space not far from where Edgar was to address the crowd. Every time Edgar looked out to the crowd he could not help but see a giant sign with the words "Remember Beltway!" Edgar, a rising political star in the Illinois Re- publican Party organization, was eager to make a good impression on some Chicago neighborhood activists, and a representative from his office contacted the group the following day. Arthur Straub chuckles at the memory: "Now the next day they called and said they would put us on a waiting list." For the next 15 years, "one or the two of us went to anything that had to do with libraries in the city." As people with grown children, Arthur and the others could make the time to drive downtown and attend evening meetings. The small, determined group of activists became regulars at public meetings where one or two of them would seat themselves at the back of the room with signs that read "Remember Beltway." Lydia Donovan remembers, "After going to the meetings, we would send Edgar's office a steady stream of letters and later faxes."

In 1994, Mayor Daley cut the ribbon at the neighborhood-wide festivities celebrating the library's completion. Jim Edgar, by then the governor of Illinois, could not attend the event himself, but he did send a representative in his place. A beautiful multimillion-dollar facility with a community meeting room, vaulted glass ceilings, extensive video and book collections, beautifully equipped children's room, and full-time staff of four (twice the size of the old building staff) replaced the cramped, modest storefront operation across the street from the airport. Civic League members viewed the Beltway Branch Library building as a monument to their devotion to the community. Arthur Straub has a simple explanation for the "philosophy" that made the building possible: "We just wouldn't let them forget who we are and where we are."

In another case of civic activism, neighborhood residents came together to call for the demolition of an abandoned warehouse neighbors nicknamed "the White Elephant." Local kids regularly used the building as a "hang-out" safe from the gaze of curious adults, and grafitti artists (or "taggers") and gang members constantly vandalized it. One editorial in the *Southwest News Herald* described the structure as an "albatross" and "a seven-story eyesore." "Deserted buildings such as these are a blight on the community. They do nothing to enhance our neighborhood. They become breeding grounds for rodents and crime as well...the Alderman can't wave a wand and make the building vanish. All he can do is keep pushing for demolition and we will keep pushing too." When the Beltway Civic League leadership joined the battle against the building, Ron Zalinsky and others made contacts with the neighborhood relations aides at the congressman's, alderman's, and mayor's offices. All three aides were accustomed to Ron's regular calls, and all knew Ron by name. BCL members remark that "it's great" being Ron's neighbor, "'cause you know your street will be the first one plowed." In no time, BCL members had used their political networks to track down the "White Elephant's" elusive out-of-state owners. Neighborhood activists also managed to navigate the city's massive bureaucracy and obtuse regulatory system to demand a public hearing in the Cook County Housing Court. The BCL then arranged for buses to transport 20 residents to attend the two days of hearings so that city officials, in Ron's words, could "see we mean business" and recognize the neighborhood's considerable resources when it comes to "people power." Just a few months later the alderman, congressman, and assorted BCL members were present when the bulldozers arrived to start demolition.

Given local activists' intense devotion to the visual landscape, it is not surprising that garden dwellers see graffiti as a violation, a symbolic assault on their way of life. "The profusion of graffiti on neighborhood buildings adds to working-class whites' visual estrangement. Some cosmopolitans read graffiti therapeutically as a symptom of urban alienation or aesthetically as minority art nouveau, a primitivism broken free of stuffy formalism," writes the sociologist Jonathan Rieder. However, to working-class urban dwellers graffiti "marked sinister forces crossing the line between public rules and private whim. Even the picturesque examples struck many as the acts of predators who violated the rules of place that reassure pedestrians in anonymous urban spaces." For the people of Beltway, in Rieder's words, "the defacement seemed to show a willingness to defy the unstated rituals that underlie the impression that 'everything is okay here.' They translated the ugly scrawls and obscenities as a form of sensory mayhem carried out against the public."[14] What Beltway's inhabitants fear most is disorder. Any graffiti are unsettling because they undermine hard-won lower-middle- and work-ing- class lives that are not only precious but also fragile.

The Southwest News Herald's police log column makes regular reports on the arrests of local vandals. One story commended a neighborhood beat officer for stopping a group of teenagers later identified as members of a notorious tagger crew. The officer approached the youngsters when he noticed paint staining their hands and clothes. Another newspaper account commended the swift action of a police officer who apprehended some teenagers "in the act" of defacing a bus alcove with paint markers. During Civic League meetings and community beat meetings, the graffiti problem is a recurring topic of heated discussion. Frustrated residents press the police "to do something" about these young criminals. Neighbors complain that teenagers have no "respect for the pride in the ownership of things." Other residents demand to know why vandalism is a lowly misdemeanor property crime that usually requires no prison time. "These kids should be locked up." "The city council needs to change the law," residents complain. When a 17-year-old American high school student was arrested in Singapore for vandalism, the penalty under Singapore's legal system—caning—created an international outcry among human rights activists who viewed the punishment as cruel and inhumane. In Beltway, neighbors privately wondered if a similar law in the United States would send wayward young people the right message about the importance of respecting property.

Mayor Daley has made the graffiti fight a centerpiece of his administration through the highly successful "Graffiti Busters" Program. At no cost to property owners, Streets and Sanitation workers will remove graffiti from any private property within the city limits. Graffiti Buster trucks are a regular sight around the neighborhood. Giant power hoses, the kind firefighters use, spray a foamy mixture onto brick walls and signs, and the offending paint magically washes away. For smaller jobs, the city dispatches work crews to paint over graffiti or wash them off by hand. When a property owner fails to act quickly to remove graffiti, concerned neighbors may dispatch precinct captains to speak with the derelict owner.

For some concerned Beltway adults, the solution to the graffiti problem lies in teaching young people to respect property. One mother wrote an impassioned letter to the *Southwest News Herald* calling on her neighbors to teach children to take pride in their surroundings. "As I look around the neighborhoods here on the Southwest Side, I am discouraged every day. The rise in the buildings being vandalized with the childish scrawl of our youth (also known as graffiti) is very distressing. I am the mother of three sons and I am pleading with the community to please take some responsibility in fighting back against this urban plague. It is our responsibility as parents to teach our children from infancy on up that violating someone else's property is just not appropriate behavior....Children must be taught the value of respecting property."

Beltway's newest arrivals, second- and third-generation Mexican Americans who have just made the leap from the crowded three-flats shared with extended kin to the luxurious privacy of the pretty brick bungalows, people like Teresa and Bobby Ochoa, are acutely aware of the links between graffiti and out-of-control kids. Hispanics, like their white neighbors, read the neighborhood's ordered landscape and declare, "It's a nice place to raise kids, and the area is safe from gangs." They insist, "You can tell how good the neighborhood is 'cause it's so clean and you can't see graffiti anywhere." Newcomers like the Ochoas abhor graffiti as much as, if not more than their white neighbors because experience in "bad" neighborhoods has given them first-hand experience with communities that have succumbed to decay and disorder. Teresa Ochoa says, "I've held kids in my arms while they were lying shot, bleeding in the street." The appearance of graffiti is the first sign that the gangs are moving in, and people like the Ochoas believe that neighbors can fight back by removing them. Bobby Ochoa does not wait for the Streets and Sanitation crews to remove graffiti along his block. He uses his own painting supplies to cover up Two-Sixers' tagging himself.

In neighborhoods throughout Chicago, and indeed throughout the nation, "tagging" is a flashpoint for conflict between kids and adults. Young people deface walls and street signs in defiant and stylized acts of opposition. Taggers violate the ordered appearance of the landscape adults work so diligently to maintain. The British cultural sociologist Dick Hedbige describes graffiti as one example of a kind of "magical"— in other words transcendent—youthful act of revolt.[15] Young people are drawn to tagging through a massive underground subculture disseminated in cyberspace and magazines. Tagging started as an urban phenomenon loosely connected to the hip-hop scene in New York that seeks to elevate the criminal to the artistic (or at least aesthetic). Tagging crews and individual taggers earn respect and admiration from their peers by "throwing up" elaborate creations on dangerous, hard-to-reach locations like subway cars and elevated bridges. The tags themselves often require a high degree of skill that only disciples of tagging can appreciate. But neighborhood residents, both young and old, understand that tagging disrespects the controlled and ordered environment the garden represents. When taggers are apprehended, it is not surprising that local residents view such criminals as saboteurs attacking their way of life.

The case of 17-year-old Orlando Santos, who was arrested vandalizing the windows of a neighborhood elementary school, immediately galvanized community residents. An off-duty police officer living near the Gerald School happened to look out his window one night and see three boys, one of them Orlando, carving the tag "SONE" into the windows of the school with a penknife. One boy managed to elude the police, but two other teenagers including Orlando were arrested. The police officer from the neighborhood, who was on a medical leave because of an injury, managed to chase the boys down a back alley. Orlando was the only one of the three from Beltway. One boy lived in the suburbs, and another lived in a neighborhood just east of Beltway.

Almost immediately, neighbors focused their anger and frustration on Santos. In the words of one resident, Orlando "is from the neighborhood. His sister even goes to Gerald's pre-kindergarten." To the Santoses' neighbors Orlando's actions represented a terrible betrayal. Bob Lahey, one of the neighbors, recalls "I mean it's bad enough doing something like that, but in your own neighborhood for chrissakes." Gerald School Principal Jean Sidwell would have preferred to handle the matter privately. However, when Orlando and his family refused to take responsibility, the principal had no choice but to contact an attorney and enlist parents and local residents in support of the school. Shortly after Orlando's arrest, over 40 parents attended a local school council meeting to discuss how the school should proceed. The Gerald School families were angry that Orlando and his family had refused to pay $1,500 needed to replace the windows.

Fearing that Santos was a first-time offender with no record who would walk away with nothing more than a slap on the wrist, concerned neighbors, Mrs. Sidwell, and a group of parents developed a plan to mobilize the community. First, families from the Gerald School arranged for cars to transport neighbors to attend Orlando's court dates "in order to put pressure on the judge" and "show that we as a community view Orlando's actions as a serious act against the community." Parents declared, "We need to start sticking up for ourselves." The judge needs to realize "that this community wants something done. If we put pressure on the judge and Santos has to pay restitution, his friends will find out he had to pay and kids will think twice." The police officer who helped capture Orlando said, "A show of force will have an impact on the kid and his family."

In time, both Orlando and his parents became targets for frustrated neighbors. Neighbors talked about how Maria Santos had pretended not to know English as she spoke with the police in an effort to delay her son's arrest. Other neighbors talked about the Santoses' new house with the $15,000 garage and speculated that the family could easily afford to pay for the windows. Some people mentioned that Orlando attended a private school. Neighbors marveled at how a boy from a home that seemed so upstanding could have been involved in such a crime. To many residents, Orlando's actions would have made more sense if he had been poor and lived in one of the poorer neighborhoods to the east.

When Orlando finally had his day in court, Mrs. Sidwell and the Gerald School parents were correct to fear that a lenient judge would dismiss the case. School was closed and city offices were running with skeletal staffs because of a blizzard. Mrs. Sidwell and ten parents and neighbors met at the school to carpool the delegation over to the tiny South Side courthouse. People like Joan and Lenny Bursik came to the hearing even though they had no children at Gerald because "we are just neighbors to the school." Mrs. Sidwell's presence that day itself was particularly noteworthy. Not only was school canceled, but she was just weeks away from having surgery on her hip. As she used her cane to navigate the icy, unshoveled sidewalk, one could not help but marvel at her and the other residents' resolve.

The court itself was a hive of activity in spite of the snow. Defendants treated their trials with a surprising degree of casualness. Most of the kids appearing before the judge were dressed in jeans and Starter jackets, and few had their parents accompanying them. Often the complainants—usually the managers of department stores connected to shoplifting cases—had not even come to court to testify. Each case that appeared before Orlando's was dismissed in a matter of minutes. There would be a brief speech from the judge about how "lucky" the defendant was to be receiving such "lenient" treatment. Carl Murphy observed the assembly-line justice and mused, "I suppose the public defender thinks he can cut some deal. Hell, I take the whole thing personally. I wouldn't be taking time off from work to see him let go. I want to have him pay the money back for the windows and for it to go on his record. It'll teach any other kids who have the same ideas. We will defend our property if we have to."

When Orlando's case was finally called, a visibly shaken Orlando, dressed in a jacket and accompanied by his parents, made his way to the bench. Mrs. Sidwell, the ten neighbors, and their lawyer followed the Santoses in silence. As the group made their way to front of the court, the judge appeared unsettled by the crowd suddenly assembled before him. When he asked, "Who is the complainant?" everyone from the

Gerald School answered in unison, "We are." Though the judge shooed the Beltway neighbors back to their seats on the wooden benches, what appeared to be simply a misdemeanor case had become a considerably more complex matter. The judge quickly agreed to the public defender's request for the case to go to trial, and yet another court date was set for a month later.

Six of the original ten neighbors made the trip to downtown Chicago for the final trial. This time a new judge named Frank Leary would hear the case. Judge Leary invited the Santoses, their attorney, the prosecutor, and the school's attorney into chambers to discuss the matter. Several minutes later, they all emerged. Orlando and his parents avoided the gaze of their neighbors as they stood before the judge to hear his decision. Judge Leary began, "Orlando, did you cause criminal damage to the school on the night of October 22nd?" Orlando in a soft voice murmured, "Yes." The public defender added, "My client is pleading guilty, Your Honor." The judge asked Orlando, "You understand that pleading guilty that you are waiving your rights and that with a class A misdemeanor you may be sentenced to up to one year in prison." Orlando's voice was even more muffled, but once again he answered, "Yes." "You are standing here before me," the judge continued, "with no previous convictions and your parents are with you so they are obviously concerned. Tell me why you did it?" Orlando simply said, "I don't know." Judge Leary turned to the Santoses. "What do you think of all this?" Mrs. Santos said nothing, but Mr. Santos responded, "We were surprised and shocked, Your Honor." Again Judge Leary asked why Orlando had vandalized the building, and yet again the boy had no answer. Orlando just shrugged his shoulders. With that Judge Leary announced his final ruling: "Now I don't think you are putting on an act for me, I think you are embarrassed at what you did and rightly so. It was a very stupid and thoughtless act. I'm going to find you guilty of causing criminal damage, which is a misdemeanor. Now Orlando, what you did was wrong. I think you are contrite and embarrassed about what you did. But just going out and destroying the windows on the school.... People in this neighborhood depend on this school. People that are worse off than you. People that can't afford private school. And then you go and do this. It's no wonder that people are moving to the suburbs, it's to get away from people like you. No wonder that people are worried that the community is going to pieces. It gets people like these right in the heart, they work to keep the neighborhood as best they can." The judge ordered Orlando to serve one hundred hours of community service and pay the $1,500 needed to repair the windows (which he did). With the verdict, the Gerald School supporters punched the air with their fists and murmured "yes" under their breath. "We got everything we wanted." "It took a long time, but now these punks will think twice before messing with the school." "We showed them we won't take any of that shit." "That'll teach 'em to go around and mess with our property." They were jubilant; they had restored order and made an example of a young person who failed to show proper reverence for the garden's distinctive sense of place. Some months later the Santos family moved out of Beltway.

Orlando Santos had come to represent all young people—and indeed all the destructive forces—which pose a threat to Beltway's ordered landscape. By damaging the windows Orlando betrayed his neighbors who "work to keep the neighborhood as best they can." This youthful and thoughtless act of destruction is akin to stabbing his neighbors in the heart in the words of the judge. The fact that he lived in the neighborhood and his own sister attended the school made the crime even more heinous. Local activists and neighbors wanted to punish Santos as a warning to other youthful miscreants about the repercussions of "messing with our property." No doubt racist assumptions about Hispanic troublemakers colored how some residents regarded the incident. Orlando and his family are part of the first wave of Mexican Americans to settle in a predominantly white neighborhood. Yet it is difficult to assess how much race played a role in residents' reaction to the incident. Racism resides comfortably in the day-to-day lives of most Americans; the people of Beltway are no exception. Racist assumptions and interpretations are regularly used to make sense of the hows and whys of occurrences in the social world, and no doubt race and racism can partly explain why neighbors were so determined to punish Orlando and his family. What is more interesting and provocative about Orlando's crime is how this minor act of vandalism came to represent such a serious offense to local activists. Clearly the Santos case is unique because neighbors had the opportunity to punish a vandal, the perpetrator of a crime that few are ever arrested for. Residents' fury about the vandalism of the Gerald School is quite consistent with anxiety over graffiti and the so-called graffiti fight.

Beltway neighbors labor to protect their position on the fringes of the American Dream, and disorder, even the most minor cases, pulls garden dwellers uncomfortably close to the dilapidated poverty that generations of the white working class have worked so hard to keep at bay. The Santos family tried to defend their son from the zealous efforts of their neighbors who sought to punish him for what many would have considered little more than a childish prank. And herein lies the source of the conflict between the Santoses and their neighbors. To the people of the neighborhood, what Orlando did is no trivial act, it is an assault on decent, hardworking people's way of life. Orlando's actions represent nothing less than treason against the garden's precious and fragile sense of place.

Gang graffiti may be difficult to distinguish from its more innocuous cousin "tagging" (for which Orlando Santos was arrested). Yet gang graffiti, unlike tagging, can be like a cancerous malignancy. Left unchecked, these earliest symptoms of gang activity may spread and become a scourge on community life. In Chicago, gang members use gang tags to carve up territory, declare wars and allegiances, and as makeshift "No trespassing" signs warning rival gang members that they may have wandered into hostile territory. With an ever-changing and highly elaborate system of graffiti, gangs mock one another by disrespecting signs—turning letters around, breaking up a star, or adding the letter "K" to the end of a tag to indicate that it was done by a "TWO-SIXER-killer," not a member of the gang.

In fact, neighbors' efficient efforts to remove graffiti had the unforeseen consequence of masking the symptoms of increasing levels of gang activity in Beltway. Rather than dealing with the kids involved in gangs, Beltwayites erased the evidence of local gangbanger activity. Indeed gang graffiti disappeared as quickly as vandals could throw up tags, and most neighbors had neither the time nor the knowledge to see that much of the vandalism was not the more benign form of tagging, but rather the handiwork of Popes gang members, who were using the tags to claim Beltway as their territory. Neighbors had assumed they were protecting Beltway from the threat of vandals and graffiti. Instead, Beltway's adult residents were turning away from the reality of growing numbers of angry, frustrated kids alienated from the idyllic possibilities of the last garden.

THE POWELL AND HARVEY
MURDERS: POINT OF NO RETURN

Just one week before Christmas in 1995, the Beltway neighborhood was shaken to its very core when 13-year-olds Melissa Harvey and Teresa Powell were murdered as they sat in a van outside the Mariah Hastings School.[16] The nightmare of gang violence had finally touched Beltway's homeowners and activists who had worked so hard to fortify the neighborhood against it. In the neighborhood consciousness (despite the improving nature of race relations) Beltway's working-class residents believe poor ghetto kids pose the greatest threat to local residents' claims to the good life. In these racist nightmares, out-of-control gangbangers would terrorize the neighborhood with open-air drug dealing and drive-by shootings. Over time, the good, decent people would be driven out. It was a familiar tale in the folklore of working-class urban dwellers.

The news of the Powell-Harvey killings shattered last-garden dwellers' dream of the perfect existence. The fact that such violence had finally touched the community was not as surprising as the details surrounding the murders. It was the revelations about who was responsible for the killings that no one in Beltway—except possibly the neighborhood's young people—could have possibly imagined.

Teresa Powell and Melissa Harvey had grown up in Beltway. The murders took place on the street in front of Beltway's Hastings School, just beyond the school playground. The Hastings School is the best public school in the neighborhood, and residents consider the residential area around the school to be one of the most desirable sections to live.

The two girls were sitting in a van talking to some older boys when they were shot. Neither Harvey nor Powell had been the intended target. The girls had made the tragic mistake of being caught in the middle of a battle over gang turf. When it was over, two white members of the Broadway Lords gang walked away unharmed, but Harvey and Powell died immediately from gunshot wounds to the face and head.

In Chicago, gang violence is such an everyday occurrence that many incidents hardly make the evening news. Beltwayites, like all Chicagoans, are certainly not oblivious to the existence of gangs; dozens of gangs operate throughout the city's metropolitan area. What shocked and disturbed Beltwayites—beyond the tragedy of two innocent girls losing their lives—was the individuals who had set these events in motion. Within hours of the murders, police arrested five boys ranging in age from 15 to 19. All five youngsters were from Beltway. All five were white. The triggerman, the son of a Chicago police officer, was just 15 years old at the time of his arrest. Thomas Costello, the son of a Chicago firefighter, was also arrested in connection with the killings. Both were later charged as adults and sentenced to life in prison. Both boys lived at home with both their parents in the pretty brick bungalows and attended private Catholic schools. Investigators later determined that the gun used in the killings was a stolen police revolver.

The story made front-page headlines in a city hardened to the realities of gang violence. A *Chicago Tribune* headline proclaimed, "A Lesson from Beltway: No Area Safe from Gangs." Another headline read simply: "Beltway Rocked." One story featured a striking photograph of the president of the Beltway Civic League, Ron Zalinsky, dressed in a respectable cap and wool overcoat, standing in front of a wall scrawled with gang graffiti. Over the photograph was the headline, "Point of No Return." The juxtaposition symbolized a battle between decent working-class values and violent kids for control of the neighborhood and its future. All the stories described the irony that homeowners had moved to Beltway to escape the violence and gangs associated with the more troubled sections of the city. In the end, it seemed that even this solidly working-class and predominantly white neighborhood could not guarantee the safety of its children from gangs and violence. At the same time, residents' unwillingness to see the Popes as a vicious street gang may have resulted in part from the disturbing parallels adult residents recognize between the behavior of the gangs and the statements of community leaders. One wonders if young people did not listen to the bold talk and bluster about defending the neighborhood and take things into their own hands. One could argue that the Popes learned about protecting turf from adults and that in many ways these gang members are far more the sons of Beltway than anyone wants to admit.

Every television report and newspaper account included yearbook photos of the two victims and made frequent mention of the fact that the murderers were white and from solidly "middle-class" backgrounds. The press and the public's interest in this case grew out of the unnerving sense that these murders were different. Such differences unsettled Chicagoans—of all races and classes—who were accustomed to linking particular notions of race and class to their understandings of gangs, violence, and crime.

News accounts took pains to describe Beltway as "a cops' neighborhood" and as "a place where gangs and crime were invaders that periodically infiltrated a peaceful oasis of beautifully manicured lawns and brick bungalows." The vast majority of adult residents complacently believed that gangs were an external problem created by outsiders (that is, lower-class Hispanic and African American youngsters from high-crime neighborhoods to the east or the poor suburb of Mountain Ridge).

The only people in the neighborhood who were not surprised by the murders were the local youngsters. Neighborhood kids knew all about the Popes, Disciples, Two-Sixers, and Latin Kings long before the murders. They could have told you how the Popes and their "wannabe" members regularly hung out in the bowling alley near the high school. They could have translated the gang tags that lined Third Avenue and that were scrawled on the abandoned factories not far from the railroad tracks. They knew all about the Pirates baseball caps and blue and black colored clothing Popes' gang members had a predilection for wearing. They could have told you that the gang's name "Popes" stands for: "*P*rotecting *O*ur *P*eople *E*liminating *S*pics, *S*pooks, or *S*cum" depending on the interpretation of the "s." They could even have shown you how to make the hand signals gangbangers "flash" to identify themselves as friend or foe. But no one ever seemed to ask the neighborhood kids. In the end, the only people in Beltway blind to the fact that gangs were not outsiders who periodically invaded the neighborhood were adults. It was as if the garden's adult inhabitants had been lulled to sleep by their hard-fought claims of lower-middle-class respectability, sturdy brick houses, well-kept lawns, and "good" families headed by police officers and firefighters. Denial and fear over losing their claim to the appearance of order and abundance forced garden dwellers to close their eyes to the problems that lurked in their own homes and neighborhood.[17]

In the days immediately following the murders, students at the Hastings School wandered around the hallways in a sort of haze. Students talked about being afraid to play in the schoolyard and around the neighborhood. In a community where neighbors often "forgot" they lived in the city, the killings became terrifying reminders of the dark side of urban life. As youngsters cried and embraced one another as they searched for comfort, one boy, a friend to one of the girls, drew a picture of two headstones with Teresa's and Melissa's names on them. In the drawing the two headstones are surrounded by flowers. On the top of the picture are the words "We miss you and we love you." The boy brought the picture to Lydia Donovan, the head librarian of the Beltway branch of the Chicago Public Library, and she displayed the drawing on the front door of the library for several weeks. Not far from where the girls were shot, on the back steps of the Hastings School, students and neighborhood residents left flowers, cards, and toys, erecting a makeshift shrine. Neighbors and family members soon purchased a granite memorial for the girls, and it was placed just below the flagpole on the school grounds.

As Beltway reeled from the news, neighbors were incapable of speaking about the circumstances surrounding the murders. Residents avoided both describing the girls' deaths as murders and discussing the Popes and the area's gang problem. In a neighborhood where residents could mobilize so effectively to combat graffiti, the existence of local gangs left people oddly mute and frozen. At the memorial service for the two girls held at St. Martin's parish just days after the killings, the teachers, family, and clergy who addressed the mourners never mentioned the violent nature of the girls' deaths. It was almost as if the girls had been struck by a car or hit by lightning, one mourner later recalled. No one talked about guns, gang violence, or young people. At the community meetings held throughout the neighborhood in the following weeks, residents continued to avoid speaking about the circumstances of the murder. Even the police only cryptically referred to the "recent incident in the neighborhood." Neighbors insisted that the killings were an isolated incident. Even when confronted with the identities of the murderers, residents continued to insist that outsider gang influences must of have played a part in the tragedy. They could not acknowledge that the Popes lived in *their* neighborhood. More stunning was the way some residents continued to deny the existence of gangs in Beltway, and others felt that the Popes were not a "serious problem."

Laura McCreesh, the principal of the Hastings School, believes residents were simply incapable of believing in the existence of local white gang members. "I think that a lot of people were naïve in this neighborhood, not believing that this exists within their community. Even at the community

forum we had people who came up and insisted that 'No, we don't have gangs in this area.' Everybody went, 'Whoa, how can you say that!' when an incident like that happened. We still have people who don't want to believe it." Mrs. McCreesh believes parents simply were blind to what neighborhood children were doing. "It was as if [the adults] don't know what they are seeing." Parents would "see a bunch of guys walking down the street with baseball bats, they don't know if they are looking at a Little League baseball team or a group of gangbangers." The comments of one mother were typical of those residents who found it difficult to accept that the Popes posed a serious threat to the neighborhood: the murders have heightened "my awareness but am I more concerned? [I would say no.]....
[To tell you the truth], I am more concerned about the kids from the high school—from other neighborhoods—who walk through [Beltway] on the way to the bus. I know these kids in the Almighty Popes. Is *that* a gang? My son knows some of them. What I see on television, you know with the Mexicans and the blacks killing each other, that's a serious problem. To me it seems like these gangs out here are just bull-s-h-i-t gangs in comparison."

In the winter of 1993, over two years before the Powell and Harvey shootings, the principal of the Hastings School hosted a gang awareness workshop for parents on how to recognize if one's child was involved with gangs. At that time, the principal was aware of Popes activity in the school and the neighborhood. The gang workshop had abysmal attendance. In April 1993, two years before the murders, the Beltway Civic League invited a neighborhood beat officer, Paul Otis, to speak at the group's monthly meeting. Officer Otis nearly caused a riot when he told the mostly senior crowd that there were a number of gangs that operated in the neighborhood, and that there had been a number of assaults and shootings in the area. When one Civic League member asked, "Where the gangs are coming from?" Officer Otis blamed suburban, Hispanic teenagers from Mountain Ridge, but he then proceeded to name several known gang members who lived in the neighborhood. As the policeman spoke, Civic League members shook their heads in disbelief, turned to each other in horror, and wondered "How can this be?"

Some people actually grabbed their chests and covered their mouths as Otis described the details of a drive-by shooting in the eastern section of Beltway. And yet, at the time of the Powell and Harvey shootings, the president of the Civic League continued to insist that he had not been aware of a local gang problem.

In the months that followed, a group of neighbors came together with local police officials to form a neighborhood watch.[18] Police officers living in Beltway used their connections to speed up the city's "problem solving" community policing initiative. Trainers originally scheduled to arrive in Beltway sometime in the late spring moved up their training program and started working with neighborhood activists by the new year. However, the community policing facilitators offered little advice for dealing with gangs. Indeed the "problem solving" approach's success rests largely on carefully selecting solvable neighborhood problems. In the words of one police department facilitator, "Gangs and drugs are big problems we really can't hope to solve here; we can try to figure out what to do about a bad corner or a business...the 'problem solving' approach can't take on these huge issues." Community activists were soon logging graffiti, filing complaints with the city because of nuisance businesses, and forming a neighborhood watch. Beltway's talented local activists raised money for walkie-talkies and T-shirts through buffet dinners, raffles, and bowling nights. Local business owners donated the funds to display ten-foot-long banners commemorating the founding of Beltway's new neighborhood watch. The banners were suspended from streetlights along Third Avenue. The neighborhood watch's new president was interviewed for a local television program showcasing successful community policing initiatives. Ultimately though, big problems like kids, violence, gangs, guns, and drugs faded into the background as activists returned to their strategy of caring for the neighborhood by focusing on the visual landscape. The police rounded up all the members of the Popes. As the gang's leadership sat in jail, the younger "wannabes" just drifted away. By the spring of 1996, local police declared that they had eradicated the Popes.

Life has moved on for the people of Beltway, and the murders have faded from the neighborhood's collective memory. While Beltwayites can no longer claim that gangs do not exist in their corner of Chicago, they insist the gangs are now gone and things are "under control." Local activists continue to battle graffiti; by 1999, they had logged and removed over 500 pieces of graffiti. Residents say graffiti are removed even more quickly now in the wake of the shootings. There is a more guarded comfort about the neighborhood. In the words of one Hastings School parent, "Everything is quiet, until the next thing happens."

◆　　◆　　◆

Over the years, Beltway residents have skillfully fought zoning issues, low-income housing developments, and graffiti. Local activists lobbied for stricter controls on local polluters from nearby factories. Neighbors waged a 15-year battle to build a new library. Indeed, Beltwayites take such great pride in their community that they regularly take the graffiti fight into their own hands because they are too impatient to wait for Streets and Sanitation to do the job. And in this place, where so many neighbors invest so much of themselves in the care of their community and homes, the Powell and Harvey killings left local activists and neighbors immobilized. Residents could barely discuss the details of the incident in public. Without a strategy for explaining how the killings had happened, activists were unable to create a line of action in response. As one mother admitted privately, "It would have been easier if the [murderers] had come from someplace else." What she meant of course is that it would have been easier if the killers had been poor and nonwhite. People struggled to make sense of the killings. "Where are the parents?" some neighbors demanded. Moralistic interpretations focused on the breakdown of young people's values. Neighbors whispered lurid speculations about what two young girls would be doing in a van with teenage boys. Neighbors tried to blame the school's lax security policies. Some said that the police should be made accountable for not doing something about the Popes before the shootings. A bizarre denial permeated much of the public discussion, as there were residents who continued to deny the existence of the Popes. Some neighbors refused to believe that local kids from seemingly good homes, blessed with all the advantages lower-middle-class respectability affords, could be responsible for a vicious double murder. In one instance, a neighbor claimed to sympathize with the Popes' efforts to protect the neighborhood from outsiders. Some residents tried to blame the victims by suggesting that the Lords gang had brought this violence upon themselves by coming to the neighborhood and asking for trouble. There were no voices demanding that the community at large examine its own culpability in the murders. As neighbors searched for someone to blame, few people called for Beltway's residents and leaders to ask difficult questions about how adults had failed the neighborhood's young people and what was not working within the community to allow kids to act out in such a way. While the killings were extreme and unusual, the existence of a critical mass of young people so alienated and destructive should have forced people to ask themselves "What can we do?" and "How have we abandoned our children?" In the end, the residents of Beltway, people who have worked hard and invested so much of themselves in their precious way of life, could not imagine that they may have unwittingly played some part in causing the tragedy.

Beyond the obvious sorrow of two young girls being killed in front of their school, the Powell-Harvey killings deeply troubled Beltway's hard-working and respectable white working- and lower-middle-class population because the ordered landscape of the garden was supposed to have protected them from the chaos gang violence represents. Swept stoops, graffiti-free alleys, and manicured lawns were the totems that magically guarded them from the dangers of urban life. Beltwayites' hubris allowed them to believe that the perverted values of ghetto dwellers perpetuated by welfare dependency, poverty, and female-headed households create crime and gangs. Perceptions of clean and dirty, dangerous and safe, and good and bad filtered through lenses of race and class made Beltwayites assume that chaos and crime result from social pathologies that only plague poor minorities. The sons and daughters of white, solidly lower-middle-class people, living with both parents, are supposed to be safe from the dangers of street life that ensnare so many young people trapped in the ghetto. Few residents had taken the members of the Popes, Satan's Disciples, or Two-Sixers seriously. "Hardcore gangbangers live in the projects," parents and neighbors assured themselves. They insisted, "The troublemakers are coming in from other neighborhoods." Even as homeowners scrubbed the gang graffiti off their garage doors, they clung to the notion that gangs only periodically invaded their community. Neighbors wholeheartedly and blindly believed in the myth of the last garden as a precious place that must be defended from outside forces. Beltwayites had never allowed themselves to see that the most serious threats posed to their way of life could come from their own children. Gangbangers cannot be white, clean-cut kids. The truth of the Popes' existence and their propensity for violence ripped at the convictions that brought the last garden to life. Self-righteous indignation about less deserving people whose lack of self control kept them from achieving the American Dream made garden dwellers look down on their neighbors trapped in the ghetto. In the end, the Powell and Harvey killings proved to be a chilling reminder of precisely how much the residents of the garden have in common with the residents of the ghetto. And unlike the ethos of the ghetto, white working-class respectability offers no room for sociological truths to explain how kids are pushed into the dangerous world of life on the streets. Beltway's families had no history of racial oppression, concentrated poverty, segregation, social pathology, or blocked opportunities to blame for why these children had lost their way. Beltwayites believe in individual responsibility when they talk about what is wrong with welfare, affirmative action, and crime in the streets. The same rules had to apply when talking about white kids living in the brick bungalows. If that is so, then the precious values that define life in the last garden had played some role in creating the evil of these killings. That truth, it seemed, was simply too much to bear.

THREE

Home, Sweet Home

Bungalows, Domesticity, and a Sense of Place

A man is not a whole and complete man
Unless he owns a house and the ground it stands on.

Walt Whitman

BUNGALOW MORALITY: KEEPING THE STREETS SAFE FOR LAWNS AND ORDER

A colleague came to me with an article he found on a recent trip to Chicago. As I read the headline that proclaimed 2001 the "Year of the Bungalow" my heart leapt. Here it seemed as if the unassuming brick bungalow, in the words of one *Chicago Tribune* reporter at least, "might be on the verge of cultural stardom." In late 2000, Mayor Richard M. Daley, who himself was raised in a bungalow, announced the Bungalow Initiative, a plan that would earmark public funds for Chicagoans who purchase or remodel bungalows. In a statement to the press, the mayor declared that "bungalows are a part of what Chicago is about" and that such housing must be protected from the onslaught of gentrification and decay. Even the distinguished Chicago Architectural Foundation (CAF) joined in the act with plans for an exhibit of models and photos that will tour the nation's libraries, historical associations, and conservatories. "Bungalows by Bus" is the most recent addition to the CAF's more conventional offerings of excursions to Frank Lloyd Wright buildings, Loop businesses, and churches. One can just imagine the bemused expressions on the faces of Bungalow Belt dwellers as they greet busloads of tourists snapping photos and debating the aesthetic merits of 1920s-era original details.

Astute political observers may accurately, albeit cynically, note that the Bungalow Initiative holds a particular appeal for Bungalow Belt dwellers notorious for voting early and often. But as Beltway's own Congressman Lipinski explains in a *Chicago Tribune* article, "Bungalow is a code word for hard-working families with strong, reliable values." According to *Tribune* reporter Mike Conklin, the significance of the bungalow, as an icon of populism and working-class values, extends far beyond the Chicago city limits, as bungalows have assumed a variety of forms throughout the United States. "The house pictured as Archie Bunker's in the opening credits of *All in the Family* is a bungalow by New York standards. The same is true of the wooden house where Richard Nixon was born in southern California."[1] This chapter considers just how the houses of Chicago's Bungalow Belt are a tangible, material expression of a distinctively working-class sensibility.

◆　◆　◆

Beltway itself looks like a sea of single-story bungalows and raised ranch–style houses.[2] The fronts, clean and neat with golden brown face brick and earth-tone vinyl siding, always look good. Walking down the street, what you see is one perfectly kept-up front after another. The effect is that of walking out on a movie sound stage where the houses are just painted fronts propped up with two-by-fours. The houses stand so low to the ground that the picture windows transform the bungalows' front rooms into fishbowls as passersby can peer in to observe their neighbors' activities. Only six feet separate the walls of neighboring houses. The pitched roofs hang over as much as 24 inches, so there is just two feet of sky between the tip of one family's bungalow and the tip of the next. Homeowners personalize their mass-produced dwellings with details like carved wood name signs, plastic geese donning gingham bonnets, lawn jockeys, gnomes, and statues of the Blessed Mother or the Infant of Prague. Because so many homeowners lay out sod every few years, the last garden's lawns look like plush green carpets from May to September. Ron Zalinsky points to his lawn and proclaims, "You see how nice it is, there are no dandelions at all, it's like a billiard table, right? Out here, everybody's got a good lawn, everybody's got their roses." For Ron, not keeping up one's lawn represents a serious moral lapse, "because if you let your outside go to pot, mostly I think the inside is gonna go to pot too."

For Halloween neighbors transform front yards into cemeteries with ghoulish headstones or suspend scarecrow-like corpses from the sides of houses. Residents hang tiny jack-o-lanterns and miniature ghosts like Christmas ornaments on their bushes or drape cobwebs on the evergreens. For Valentine's Day, the picture windows in the living room may be filled with hearts and cupids. At Easter, the hearts and cupids become Easter eggs and bunnies. The fact that Beltway is predominantly Polish, German, and Lithuanian does not prevent residents from joining in the St. Patrick's Day festivities by decorating the front windows with shamrocks and leprechauns. Even the neighborhood's newest arrivals, Mexican Americans, use their houses to tell the world to "Kiss Me, I'm Irish." The most spectacular show comes at Christmas time. Supposedly friendly competitions among neighbors escalate into full-scale wars as homeowners use thousands of colored lights to trim every free square inch of bush, tree, and roof. Gigantic plastic candy canes, light-up Santas, and life-size crèches transform dreary patches of gray, snow-covered lawns into a whimsical holiday showcase. "There are so many lights out here," says one neighbor, "that it looks like Las Vegas." Swept up in the festivity of the season, the usually clannish Beltwayites welcome people who stop to admire their handiwork.

For the working-class people of Beltway today, washing the car is a widely practiced weekly ritual. Big American cars never went out of style in Chicago's Southwest Side. Every weekend, men go out to their alleyway garages to scrub, buff, and polish every inch of their beautifully maintained made-in-the-USA Fords, Chryslers, and GMs.

The word bungalow (from *bangla* meaning of, or belonging to, Bengal) originally described any Bengali house sitting freely in a garden. In America, the term eventually came to mean a one-story dwelling with a distinctive, very low, wide pitch to the roof that was particularly popular between 1900 and 1930. In a wave of construction that started in the 1920s, followed by a second wave in the 1950s, Beltway was originally built up as part of the Bungalow Belt: "A world of tidy little one-story, single family houses extending west from the edge of the ghetto all the way to the city limits."[3] Back in 1960, you could buy a brand new house for $18,000. One decent income from the Nabisco factory was enough to pay the mortgage and still have a little something left at the end of the month.

Chicago's Southwest Side has given the Chicago bungalow its social and architectural significance. Solid, modest, and well constructed, bungalows provide an architectural metaphor for the people residing within them.[4] According to the sociologist David Halle, "Home-ownership, among the working- and lower-middle classes, is a major goal and a rarely questioned ambition. And this goal, once achieved, is seldom regretted for [a house] is freedom to do as one pleases without the restrictions a landlord might impose. There are pleasures associated with space and privacy."[5] Historian Kenneth Jackson writes, "Home-ownership is the most visible sign of having arrived at a fixed place in society, the goal to which every decent family aspires. On the simplest and most basic level, the notion of life in a private house represents stability, a kind of anchor in the heavy seas of urban life."[6] However, when working-class people talk about home-ownership, Halle continues, "it is the economic advantages, in particular the difference between what they paid for their houses and the present market value that most often come to mind."[7]

Given Beltwayites' socioeconomic position, the goal of home-ownership and, once a house is purchased, the house itself are the focal points of working-class lives. For people who earn $40,000 per year, a $140,000 house represents a major financial commitment.[8] And unlike making other financial investments, like CDs, savings accounts, or stocks and bonds, purchasing a house is charged with meaning. Becoming a home-owner is the American Dream's most conspicuous rite of passage.[9] Other indicators of status, like a college degree or a job promotion, do not take on a physical form the way a house does. You do not simply use or consume a house; it is where you eat, sleep, search for comfort, and care for children. When you are gone, it may be the only thing you leave behind in this world. It is not surprising then that the displays of housepride become self-conscious, and sometimes over-the-top, demonstrations of abundance and order that reinforce an individual's social and cultural place in the world.

Home-ownership also serves as a clear social marker that separates hardworking, contributing members of the community from the more transient and shiftless ones. In the experience of working-class home-owners, less-deserving elements—specifically renters, lower-class whites and minorities, and other "bad" neighbors—possess neither the economic resources nor the moral rectitude to commit themselves to the collective interests of the wider community. The fastidious upkeep of lawns and houses is inextricably linked to homeowners' ongoing efforts to establish, and also insulate, their social status. Solicitousness of property, the homogenous architecture, and this fetishistic concern for cleanliness become weapons that defend homeowners from the chaotic forces of crime, poverty, and disorder that threaten precarious working-class lives.

The cornerstone of working-class urban whites' racism is the fear that racial turnover threatens property values. Because the equity in a house is a working-class family's primary form of savings, the loss of $10,000 in a house's resale value represents a major threat to a family's economic security. More affluent property owners have access to social status and financial assets that make them less risk averse to the possibility of living in close physical proximity to the poor.[10] Similar dips in property values will not wipe out a middle- or upper-middle-class family's sole source of wealth. Working-class homeowners' socioeconomic vulnerability heightens awareness about the risks created by living in close proximity to lower-class populations. Because it is not possible for working-class homeowners to distance themselves physically or economically from poverty, they create *symbolic* distances and erect *moral* boundaries instead. By strengthening such place-bound moral distinctions between "good and bad neighbors," the people of Beltway reassure themselves and make it clear to the rest of the world that they are fundamentally different from those just below them on the social ladder. Beltway's anxious homeowners will not tolerate any ambiguity about what distinguishes the garden from the ghetto.

In the logic of working-class homeowners, low-income whites and minorities have no way to appreciate how home-ownership affects the interests of all neighbors. Poor people living in housing projects or "Section 8" cannot see that an "unblemished lawn, free from weeds, dandelions, dog feces, or planted tires" and the "freshly painted house front" is a sort of tax imposed on their neighbors' behalf.[11] In the working-class world Beltwayites have created, houses and home-ownership dominate the patterns of everyday life. Fastidious homeowners lavish attention on their homes the way they might dote on a child. A gendered division of household labor also marks life in Beltway (men paint, landscape, and oversee construction projects while women handle housework and home décor). Both men and women see household labor and display as a statement about identity—in other words, one's place in the social world. In the case of women, it is not that they enjoy housework; rather it is that they appropriate housework and the appearance of the home to make social proclamations about the kind of mother, wife, and woman they are. In this way, the material world and one's possessions merge with the psyche to construct a sense of self.

RENTERS AND HOMEOWNERS

The transition from renter to homeowner is a significant economic and moral rite of passage. In the words of George Braddock, who observed many of his neighbors move from the crowded three-flats into their own homes in the 1960s, the step up to a bungalow means "people have a little more money they want something better." His wife Peggy adds, "If people wanted more space, they moved out this way." Forty-five-year-old Crystal Kaiser has lived in Beltway for most of her life. She moved out to Beltway with her first-generation Polish American parents over three decades ago. Her family's story is typical. "A lot of people that came out here were like my parents, they were being displaced. My parents moved because the University of Illinois–Chicago campus was being built. After World War II, everyone was living in those apartments—in flats—and then everybody started moving out here into houses. It just seemed like everybody moved at the same time. My mother was a beautician and my father was a maintenance man. They bought their house for $13,000." According to retiree Harry Pashup, a longtime Beltway resident in his sixties, working-class city workers like himself moved out to Beltway because of the high quality of city services and because the purchase of a bungalow represents such a sound investment. "City workers think this is a preferential ward for them. So you can count on at least 10 percent of every block works for the city. They like Beltway because when you're investing a certain amount of money in a house, would you throw your money out the window or put it into a bank? In other words, you'd want to put your money into some property you could turn over if you had to. That's why people maintain their property out here."

Much of the Beltway Civic League's activism centers around the concerns of the area's homeowners. Indeed, one of the BCL's primary goals is to serve as a gatekeeper protecting the interests of local residents who own their homes. The BCL has led several successful campaigns to restrict the construction of multi-unit housing to the busy commercial arteries along Fifth and Third Avenues. Indeed, the West Ward alderman promised his constituents in 1995 that no new multi-family dwellings would be constructed along the side streets in close proximity to the single-family bungalows. Until recently, renters were not allowed to become members of the Civic League. When Lydia Donovan, who happens to rent her apartment, was elected president of the Civic League, she could not take office until the BCL amended its constitution. The neighborhood's school districts have been creatively gerrymandered so that children living in the apartment buildings along Fifth and Third Avenue all attend the same elementary school.

Area homeowners contend that renters are simply passing through and therefore have little incentive to be "good neighbors." One woman who owns a house not far from the apartment buildings stands out on her front step as she explains why renters are the frequent targets of local activists and concerned neighbors like herself. "The Civic League talks about how they don't want condos or rentals because most of the people that come in to rent don't remain. They may not care about dumping their garbage out or leaving beer bottles in the alley." The apartment buildings are viewed as the doorway for undesirable lower-class elements to infiltrate Beltway. Out-of-control, problem kids are created by bad parents who fail to uphold the neighborhood values for supervising children. Police and school officials say "Gangbangers don't move into a particular neighborhood on their own to set up shop, it's the parents who bring them in." Law enforcement, neighbors, and local activists view the presence of apartment buildings as a threat to the community's ongoing efforts to maintain Beltway's decent quality of life. Fears about renters are tinged with race- and class-based assumptions, but the division between renter and homeowner takes shape in Beltwayites' conceptualization of a place-bound moral order. Decency and respectability are defined in terms of one's ability to purchase and maintain property. In the words of one homeowner, "You're talking about a different kind of people [in the apartments]. People right away think like you're being prejudiced against a certain nationality. I really don't think that's it. It's all based on the same type of values. There's an apartment building across the street [populated with white renters] and the people there don't have the same type of values as the people here [on this side of the block]. They just don't." She goes on to describe how the interests of homeowners feed into the racism of working-class residents. "People around here think that the blacks who want to move in are coming in from 63rd and Western," an area of the city known as Murder Alley. "I don't blame people for feeling that way because the people here are working-class people and they work for what they have. And this is all they have. A lot of people here don't have much more than their bank accounts. They don't have a plan. This is everything to them. They are just protecting their ownership of things" when they try to keep certain groups from moving in.

In Beltway, home-ownership is as natural, expected, and desirable a goal as getting married and having children. And like marriage and children, home-ownership thus becomes an act that your neighbors can use to evaluate your moral timbre. "I grew up in the Bungalow Belt," declares Lillian Crimmins. " When I was growing up, to the west of us around Beltway was the place to live. You get married, and then you move out to a place like Beltway. If you don't have a house, what have you done with your life? Owning a house is the ultimate dream. So when you do get a house you're creating your perfect existence. And if you're not, then you're not living up to these expectations." Toni Capelevski, who lives in a pristine bungalow near some apartment buildings, insists, "Most of what people live on comes from their pocketbook, and their houses are their proof of achievement. To me, it's the most middle-class badge they have. For them, we still come from these working-class people. So to them, it's all very important. They don't have much more than their houses. This is everything." Loretta Riley, homemaker and home-owner, explains, "People are proud of their property . . . and it's like they think they're making a contribution that way."

HOUSEPROUD NEIGHBORS

Walking along the narrow sidewalk between the houses to the back lot, you notice how the narrow walkway is neatly swept and landscaped with shade plants. Every bit of lawn must be carefully kept up; even a dark, narrow corner of the house is not ignored. Indeed, neighbors will complain if people "do not take care of the side of the house facing me." The back lot itself is usually fenced off so that people cannot cut across through to the front. Because the backyards are somewhat more private, their appearance is less formal. But just as neighbors pay attention to how your children behave and your front lot looks, they also pay attention to the condition of the back. In Beltway, untidy backyards remain as rare as untidy fronts.

The back lots are only 28 x 25 feet. A common home improvement project for the man of the house is building a porch or installing a pool. The decision to build a pool determines the fate of a backyard in Beltway since, once the pool is installed, there is room for little else. If there is no pool, the backyard may become filled with a variety of gardening projects. Indeed, Beltwayites take great pride in their elaborate landscaping efforts. Massive European-style gardens with gigantic flowerbeds, roses, and topiary seem to blanket the neighborhood from spring to fall. During the summer months, residents spend hours talking over fences exchanging advice on roses and sharing tips on growing tomatoes. Beltway's most spectacular gardens feature fountains, statues, miniature gazebos, and trellises. Notably, one older resident of Dutch extraction constructed a working miniature wooden windmill.

Upon entering the typical bungalow or raised ranch, the first thing you notice is how long and narrow it is. The front door opens into a room with a large picture window facing the street. A television sits in the front living room, and the "good" furniture is on display in showroom condition. Usually you can date the decade when the living room furniture was purchased because people select the trendiest styles associated with a particular time period. Given the size of living rooms, there is space only for a coffee table, a couch, and an armchair. The colors are monochromatic, bright, and slightly feminine. Men worry about carpentry, painting, and plumbing projects. Choices about furniture and interior decoration will be left to the woman of the house. Flower-print upholstery and light colors are extremely popular. If the upholstery is blue, the carpets, walls, and wall decorations are also likely to be assorted shades of blue. In most homes, people try to make their furnishings match because things ought to look as if they were in a department store.

There is no formal dining room. The living room leads into an eat-in kitchen, and along the hallway from the living room to the back of the house are the master bedroom and bedroom(s) for the children. Most homes have finished basements that may serve as a family room, a play-room, or even a second apartment for adult children or elderly parents. The shelves in the living room are filled with bric-a-brac like tiny china figurines or decorative candles, wedding portraits, and the kind of formal baby pictures taken at department stores like Sears. Sometimes there are glass cases displaying small collectibles. Often the decorations may reflect the theme of the room. If the room has an "oriental" décor, there may be fans on the wall or a china figurine of a woman in traditional Chinese costume. If the room has a contemporary, art deco style, the decorative pieces on the walls and shelves may be sleek and black and white. Typically, there are no books on display.

Walking through the living room, one then comes upon the kitchen. Kitchens are the focal points of houses. This is where wives/mothers, husbands, and children spend most of their time, and where women do most of their entertaining. Like the living room, the kitchen is an important facet of household display. Women often talk about how they plan to improve the kitchen. Butcher-block cabinets—usually made of pressed wood or laminate—are popular. The colors in the kitchen—beige, browns, and whites—are more sedate than those in the rest of the house. Women will brighten up the kitchen area with homey touches like dried flower arrangements or pictures of fruit. Like the living room's, ideally a kitchen's décor should have a theme and things should match and look as though they fit together. It is nice to have things that are new and modern.

Beltwayites have earned a reputation for being houseproud. Indeed, residents often speak of their pride in the ownership of things. At first glance, houseproud displays might seem like nothing more than demonstrations of affluence and status. And clearly, being houseproud has elements of "showing off." For Toni Capelevski, being houseproud means that when "a conversation comes up, you do a whole description of everything that you have in your house and when you bought it and what you paid for it." Peggy Braddock describes her neighbors' houseproud behavior as an all-consuming, virtually religious sacralization of property. Indeed Peggy's comments evoke the theistic imagery of a worshipper kneeling before an altar as she describes her neighbors working on their hands and knees to cut the grass. "I'd walk to Columbia Avenue and I'd see everybody's lawn. And there are more houseproud people out here than I've ever seen. You can really tell. Some blocks, I mean every lawn is just perfect. You don't see too many where they just let it go. I mean we've got people who get down on their hands and knees with a pair of scissors. To do stuff like that takes time. But nobody just seems to let it go. They care maybe what the neighbors think of them. If somebody's got garbage all over their property and lets the weeds grow free, their neighbors don't like them."

Like any other kind of religious devotion, residents' veneration of their bungalows serves two purposes. First, by pulling the weeds, shoveling the snow, and scrubbing the vinyl siding with a brush, Beltwayites announce that they are believers and they belong to the faith. Their belief assures them a place in heaven or, in this case, their place in the Eden of the last garden. Second, this veneration serves as a kind of protection for the garden's inhabitants who live in such close social and physical proximity to the ghetto.

Franny Wertelka believes that Beltwayites' adoration of their homes, lawns, and gardens is more than status display. The neighborhood's visual landscape reflects residents' psychic connection to a distinctive way of life. "They're fanatical, they're just amazing in Beltway. I would agree with the congressman that this is the last garden. They are very, very into their lawns and their gardens and that's just important to them. It's a pride. I think people generally want to show that their houses are very important to them. Keeping the home up is part of that pride associated with that investment. I think that rings true in Beltway. I really do. They're so fanatical about little things that in some other neighborhood wouldn't seem like a big deal. But over there, it is." Toni Capelevski adds, "People around here, when they're hiring someone to do the work on their home, they tend to work right alongside them."

Houseproud displays make it possible to transform empty, meaningless physical space into a place pregnant with evocative symbolic significance. The elaborate holiday displays with gigantic Santas and the manicured lawns mark out territory and announce to the world what kind of place Beltway is and, by extension, what kind of people the residents of Beltway are. It is the sort of place where people are so committed to their property that a man would scrub the siding of his house the way someone might scrub a dirty kitchen floor. It is the kind of place where homeowners would pay to have the brickface of a bungalow professionally cleaned with high-powered jet hoses. Another neighbor reports, "Some of my neighbors, they mow the grass one day of the week and one day is for the flowers, and this is just the flowers on the one side of the house." Such extreme houseproud behavior takes shape in the fragility of working-class lives. Beltwayites have only recently (and barely) achieved their Edenic version of the American Dream. In a sense, your house owns you because this is all you can expect from the world. Former Alderman John Puchinski describes neighbors' "respect for property" as something they are raised to have. "People on the Southwest Side, we have a lot of blue-collar, strong family values type attitudes among people. People were brought up, their parents and grandparents were the same way, they were brought up to care for their property. They came from hardworking families. Their lawns are well groomed, people build decks and swimming pools. People can't afford to travel much and take big trips, so they do things around their house. Sitting outside in your backyard and having a barbecue, sitting out by the pool and having a nicely kept front and backyard. In the Southwest Side, we have a ton of block parties where neighbors get together. It's just that people have respect for their property, and, like I said, it has a lot to do with how people are brought up." The uncertainty of Beltwayites' working- and lower-middle-class status puts residents constantly on the lookout for signs that their grip on their garden may be loosening.

The concern for the outward appearance of houses also affects how residents decorate the houses' interiors. Homeowners place favorite decorations behind drapes; the result is that people passing by or looking in from across the street are the only ones who can view these items. Beltwayites decorate their houses knowing that strangers will peer in and evaluate these private, intimate spaces.

The unwritten laws that govern life in Beltway can be quite demanding. Individuals who deviate from the social norms—even on the most minor levels of clothing or appearance—can expect to be sanctioned by other members of the community. For one former resident who left the Southwest Side, "These are not worldly people. This is all they have. The ultimate dream is not getting a Ph.D. or taking a world cruise and helping other people. The ultimate dream is buying a house." The solicitousness for property belies the harsh economic truth of how seemingly comfortable lifestyles are made possible through credit cards and refinancing. In this world, consumption is no passive activity, consumption is a culturally rich enterprise that magically conjures the good life. Toni Capelevski's own house is an exquisitely maintained bungalow that still has the careful, self-conscious appearance of a showroom, which is all the more remarkable because she has teenagers. Even though Toni says she distances herself from the all-consuming consumption of many of her neighbors and friends, she claims to understand the source of such behavior. According to her, it grows out of the economic insecurities of the working-class people reaching out for middle-class status. "The peo-

ple here in the neighborhood remind me of my family and the neighborhood I came from, just on a little higher level." Toni's father is a retired factory worker, and her mother worked in a bakery. "They had to
struggle, they worried about every penny." She continues, "People around
here are very into their houses. Most people around here are remodel this,
remodel that, gotta buy this, gotta buy that. They work for their houses.
To them, it's a sign of accomplishment. Most people have houses so that
when you walk in, they want you to talk about it and compliment them
on the house. I have friends, a fireman in particular, and I'm surprised to
hear this from men but they talk about who has what and the haves and
the have nots and they're competitive about that."

Even though the elaborate lawn decorations and perfectly maintained
homes are parts of social performance produced to create a display of
affluence and status, there is also a sincere identity work that motivates
residents' devotion to their homes and possessions. Good neighbors and
other true believers do not simply fear sanctions from their neighbors.
For the devout, taking care of your home becomes central to how you
see yourself and how you want the world to see you. Here Toni
Capelevski describes the unsettling contradiction of a neighbor whose
behavior proves that she does not sincerely embrace the moral beliefs
that define Beltway's distinctive sense of place on the level of home.
"Now this neighbor, she has plastic on the furniture. You could come
into the living room on special occasions and stuff like that. Then you
delve into the family's personal life and then all these other things come
out. The whole surface of the family was clean-cut and upstanding and
then all of a sudden, out of the clouds, comes all these problems. And
now the husband is gone, they're not taking care of anything. Nobody
was cutting the lawn. But if you talked to them before, it was very important for them to tell you that they drive a nice car and they painted
their living room or that they bought new carpeting and stuff. But it was
a whole façade. You find out that they really didn't want to take care of
things or live like that that but they did it so that people would think a
certain way about them."

For wife, mother, and local dressmaker Kathy Fenton, her own experience growing up in a poor, rural town in West Virginia makes her particularly sensitive to the need to "keep up appearances." To Kathy, the appearance of her home and her neighbors' homes is so important that "the way I am, I would personally get a second job before I would let something fall apart." Kathy continues, "And I just think that if that starts happening around the area, then you can't be proud anymore—even within your own house you want to be proud of your surroundings. I grew up in an area that was extremely dilapidated, so I've seen enough." She insists, "I would leave if the neighborhood was dilapidated, if it was deteriorated to where nobody cares about the neighborhood and you start driving down the street and lawns are overgrown and doors are hanging off. I don't like to see things fall apart."

WOMEN, DOMESTICITY, AND HOUSEHOLD DISPLAY

In their houses, women use the domestic sphere and their roles as home-maker, mother, wife, property owner, and neighbor to cultivate rich social identities. The activities and labor that take place in, around, and through the house power the house's material form with cultural and symbolic electricity. The very appearance of a house becomes a manifestation of the physical and symbolic labor women do. It is as if the house embodies a woman's very identity as "good mother" and "good woman." As Clare Cooper notes, "just as the body is the most obvious manifestation and encloser of a person, so also is the home itself a representation of the individual. Although it is only a box, an often unindividualized result of mass production, it is a very particular box—an almost tangible expression of self."[12] When Teresa Ochoa describes her house, she makes it clear that she sees the humble 1930s brick bungalow as an extension of herself in her role as mother to her two young children. "Oh yes, I see the house...it's all a part of me. It's a reflection of me. My husband and I have worked so hard for this house. I am so proud of it. We really wanted a house with a basement so we could add on. And in the room over there I have walls of fame for Isabella, and little Bobby, Bobby, and me. Like I have all the kids' prizes and drawings up on the wall. Isabella's stuff from the Brownies is there and Bobby's awards from work are there too. I have my appreciation certificates from the school for my volunteer work. I want my kids to see how much I do for them. I hope it will matter to them. I wanted the room next to the kitchen to be the family room so the kids would be close to me here in the kitchen when they come home after school or if they are playing with their friends. Oh yes, this house means so much to me." For Neely Martin, whose nicely decorated house is tidy and ordered even though it is scattered with toys, "To me my house is a reflection of my life right now because I'm in it so much. This is basically why I am not working full-time because I thought kids should be in their own home growing up instead of somebody else's home. I guess, to me, it's kind of like your life is your house. I want my kids to have memories of playing in their own home instead of a babysitter's. I want them to have memories of this house." As Joyce Czawjowski talks about her house, the description seamlessly becomes a narrative about her life as a mother and wife. For Joyce, it is as if her house and her life story have fused together. "I love my house. Mostly what I think about my house is the memories, the good memories. My husband Lou and I picked things to do work on in the basement together. Stevie's communion party was in the house and we've had a lot of company over the years. The kids have had their friends over. What I'd miss most about the house if I had to leave is the memories. Lou would make his spaghetti sauce every weekend, and I remember Stevie used to get sick eating it and always on the same spot on my living room carpet. And we laughed and laughed so much about that when we were pulling out those rugs years later. It was like throwing away these memories of Stevie. If I could pick up the house, even if I had to move, I'd be happy. But it's hard to put into words. Like the one thing I miss about our old apartment, Lou and I had just been married and we did some fun things in our apartment. Even though you take the memories with you, it'd be nice to have those rooms you were in … like when you conceived your children. Just to have it as a part of you, to keep it. Just like you keep pictures that the kids do for you. That's why I say if I never move out of here, I'll be happy."

While the domestic sphere is usually assumed to be a private, closed world, working-class women in Beltway use motherhood and home-making to create social performances clearly intended for public consumption. Now a grandmother, Helen Anton recalls how a neighbor marveled at her disciplined morning routine with her young children. "I used to have a neighbor and she used to be getting up at 9 A.M. She said she'd be opening up her blinds and she'd see me walking my two youngest. … I'd be walking the two girls in the stroller. Well, my husband had to get up early for work, and I'd get the two boys up for school. If the weather was nice I would take the two little ones, I'd leave the breakfast dishes on the table, come back, and put the baby in for her nap and put the older one in front of the TV and I know I'm wrong but it was always public television so that's okay. And then I'd clean up the dishes. But my neighbor always used to say how the first thing she saw every morning was me walking down the street with those two little girls."

"When women engage in 'houseproud' or 'obsessive' behavior in order to keep a perfectly clean or tidy house, the terms are in quotation marks advisedly because they describe not so much the facts of the situation as a set of social values pertaining to them."[13] Observers may see housework as trivial and inferior work, but working-class women reclaim housework as a socially worthwhile and symbolically important endeavor. It is not that women enjoy housework, it is just that they transform housework and household display into a socially rewarding enterprise. Women dust the moldings, polish the doorknobs, scrub the floors; even areas completely hidden from view—behind refrigerators and under the sofa—get cleaned because this labor proves to the world that one is decent, clean, hardworking, and worthy. Even if the neighbor does not notice whether or not you clean behind the refrigerator, the woman of the house knows. In the domestic sphere, women have the power to look down upon a miniature world they have created for themselves and their families and the social world to behold. According to Joyce, " The first thing people notice is whether or not the house is clean and the decorating I have. It seems to me like most of the time when people come into my house, the first thing they notice is how I've decorated the kids' rooms and how everything matches...and of course, if the house is neat." Working-class homemakers do not have careers or easy opportunities for higher education. The paths to status that give their elite counterparts praise and social worth are not easily accessible. As a result, the meanings attached to housework and household display have evolved into an all-important and all-consuming strategy for earning social esteem. The devotion women have to their homes makes comparisons to the perfect display in a doll-house seem appropriate. Through this painstaking labor, women manufacture a tiny world they control absolutely. Women, as protectors of the home, literally the homemakers, build meaning in their lives by transforming these unassuming brick boxes into the expressions of themselves. In the words of Lillian Crimmins, who left life in the Southwest Side after her divorce to follow her dreams of a college degree, "These women know there is more to life but they haven't identified it yet. The house has got to be perfect or else they've failed...failed as a woman." Toni Capelevski describes the houseproud behavior of a friend. "I have a friend whose husband goes to work at more than one job and the wife has created a front room they can't go into. Then after ten years, they're going to repaint the room and get new furniture when nobody even sat in it. When you go into someone's house and they have a living room you can't go into,...[I guess] when you've struggled your whole life and you have to take hand-me-down furniture and then one day you get the new sofa and it's all yours, you don't want anybody to wrinkle it. I guess the good thing is that they don't use plastic anymore."

CLEANLINESS IS NEXT TO GODLINESS

Beltwayites never enter houses through the front door facing the street. One Beltway resident has a friendly message on her front door written in calligraphy telling visitors, "Back door friends are best." This serves two purposes. First, the back door is less formal and signifies intimacy. Second, going in through the back door means you do not walk through the formal living room, which is always neat and well maintained but is rarely used for entertaining. The interiors of the homes are always immaculate; there is none of the so-called shabby chic so popular in more affluent homes. Each stick of furniture and every piece of bric-a-brac have carefully assigned positions. There is thought, attention, and care in every detail of these homes. But cleanliness, order, and the overall appearance of a kitchen are far more important than an appliance's newness or a wallpaper's color per se. Kitchens must be immaculate. Decent, hardworking, respectable women scrub the floor every night, leave no dishes in the sink, and wipe all the crumbs off the counters. Whenever people expect company, unless they know the visitor quite well, a hostess will be sure that her kitchen is absolutely spotless.

Usually Beltwayites host guests in the kitchen or the basement. Many homeowners have finished their basements or furnished them with hand-me-downs from the living room or parents' homes. In many cases, the basements even have small kitchenettes and second bathrooms so that the good kitchen and the good bathroom do not get so much use. Because the furnishings are not new, people do not worry about kids or visitors ruining the rugs or furniture. When Beltwayites do use living rooms, they are careful to ensure that furniture is well protected. As one woman ushered me into her condominium, she made a point of showing me the couch, which was custom designed for her husband's bad back. The couch was over 40 years old. Pointing to the towels that completely hid the upholstery she said, "Do you know how this stays in such good condition? I never take the towels off for anyone. That's how it's lasted that long." Most women admit that the first thing they notice when they enter a neighbor's home and likewise the first thing the neighbors notice when they come into their homes is whether or not the house is clean. Helen Anton admits, "The first thing I notice is whether it's a pig-sty [laughter]. I don't mean, I don't mean just messy. Particularly, I understand like my neighbor, she has three young kids. And I say to her, 'Sue, I had four kids and I felt like I was forever taking care of the house.' Every 28 days Stan would change shifts and between that and the kids... I would take my husband to work and then I would clean the house while the kids slept.... [MK: If a house isn't clean, what does that say to you?] Well, either she's having a bad day, or she's lazy." At a social gathering, when I mentioned the name of a well-known community activist, another guest at the party yelled so that everyone could hear: "He's my neighbor. He's terrible. He just keeps his house in a mess. I hate him." When I noted that the family was going through a series of personal tragedies, another guest remarked impatiently, "Well, you still have to take care of things."

Neely Martin described how happy she was when her former neighbors sold their house and moved out. Not only was the house run down and dilapidated because the teenage children were allowed to run wild through the place; Neely remembers one weekend when she and her husband returned home from a trip to find this "gigantic thing, this fort completely blocking my kitchen window. It was all you could see in the backyard. Can you believe the mother had just let them do it?" Another Beltway resident, after finding graffiti on his garage, half joking and half in earnest wondered if "the neighbors spray painted my garage on purpose so that I would have to fix it up." When one man was surprised by a birthday party in his home, just moments after everyone had yelled "Surprise!" he whispered to his wife that she should have insisted he re-paint the bathroom.

As one resident took her guests on a tour of her home, she made a point of showing them the closets, for she wanted people to see how she had neatly folded and color-coordinated her linens and towels. Bobbie, a gardening enthusiast whose own backyard is filled with flowers and shrubs, complains bitterly about a neighbor three houses away whose backyard is filled with old appliances, tools, and assorted machinery. According to Bobbie, "His backyard ruins my view from the kitchen window." She longs to call the city and say she has seen rats "so the Inspector can force him to clean out that junk."

Among Beltwayites, particularly (although not exclusively) women, cleanliness is used to make judgments, indeed moral pronouncements, about one's intelligence, qualities as a parent, and decency. Joyce Czawjowski describes her neighbor's house to explain how the woman has failed in her responsibilities to herself and the rest of the community: "Well, she lives like a country person. She has about 32 bird feeders in the backyard and we have asked her a couple of times to please take them down. She's got birdseed all over and we've got mice in our backyard.... She has two cats and one is always out and he dug up my bushes.... she completely ignores me. Her big dogs urinate by the side of my house and it's ruined a few of my trees. Now her husband was very nice to me, the kids, and Lou.... Until he died, the husband would take care of the lawn. She's never been super friendly, her husband was the friendly one. [Joyce's tone changes and she becomes quite passionate.] But you know, I take care of my property. My husband is always cutting our grass. We take care of our property. We have a cat and obviously the cat is going to get out now and again. But my cat doesn't go around ruining people's bushes. My kids don't ruin her lawn. My kids have never destroyed any of her property.... Since her husband died, we've had nothing but weeds on her side. She doesn't take care of her property." Neely Martin described how she and her neighbors used cleanliness and the appearance of a house to evaluate a woman whose teenage daughter overdosed on drugs. While the neighbors sympathized with the family's tragic loss, the appearance of the family's home was used to assess the family's culpability in their daughter's death. Neely and her neighbors equated the house's shabby state with the lax parenting and weak values that contributed to the girl's descent into drugs. There is no self-consciousness about how people look into one another's windows. "There's a house down the street [where the daughter died from a drug overdose]. . . . But if you go to that house and you look inside, the house is real bad. And the yard is junky. It has this real junky swing-set on the outside. I didn't really notice until it was called to my attention. People would be talking about 'these people down there.' And I was like, 'Which house?' I really didn't notice things, but now I do. If you look in, there is nothing in there. The walls are kind of orange and there is a microwave sitting right there in the living room."

Kathy Fenton describes some bad neighbors on her block "who don't care about anything. We've got two people on the block and I really hate labeling people, putting them in a category. But they'd be considered [long pause], I'll just say they are people who don't care. They don't care about anything. Their kids in the wintertime don't have proper clothing. They don't keep up the yard. Their cars are a mess. Their house is a mess. They don't care. [MK: Are they poor?] I don't know their financial situation, but I think even if you're poor, you can be clean. You can take care of things even if you're poor. Now I always see the mother when she goes off to work and she's got a nice coat on for work and the kids are running around in torn pants and dirty clothes. I just think there's something wrong with that. You have to look nice to go to work, but your kids have to look nice too. The mother is awfully selfish, that they have their priorities backwards. When I see things like that, these people shouldn't have kids. They don't need kids. I know that people say, 'well, kids are going to get dirty.' But they don't realize they are portraying something different. When my kids walk out the door, you know, I could have the same old sweater, but they're going to go out in something nice. And if it's not new, it's clean." According to Kathy, the ability to live in filth is a window into the failure of one's moral character. "I think filth, now if you walk into a house and it's filthy. . . 'cause if somebody can live in filth it kind of gives you an idea into what the person's about. I don't care if it's messy, as long as it's clean. Now for me, somebody could have an old sofa and the most mismatched odd furniture in the world and it doesn't matter. But if a house is dirty. . . and I mean filthy— to me, it just says something about someone's character. You can have clothes thrown all over the place but if their corners are clean then they're okay. If the garbage isn't overflowing on to the floor and the kids aren't eating out of the garbage then we're okay."

Among Beltwayites, the cleanliness of a home also has an ironic valence. While people value cleanliness, neatness, and order, the appearance of a home ought not to become more important than sociability and good company. For Toni Capelevski, feeling comfortable in someone's home is singularly important. "I like a house that when I walk into it, if I feel, and this has to do with the person who owns the house and how it is decorated, if I feel like taking off my shoes and there is no problem with that. If you walk in and you want to put your feet up on the sofa, without your shoes of course, but I want to be real comfortable in a house....I go by my girlfriend Tracy's house and she asks me if I want something to drink and I just go and get it. She has no problem with that and I have no problem with that. I've had my parents come into my house and no matter where I've lived they've never been comfortable and it just breaks my heart. I have to wait on them and that makes me uncomfortable....That's what I would like. I love people to be comfortable." As Neely Martin explains, "If a house is really decorated or if it's a perfect house then you know, 'Don't step on this person's rugs.' I think that if somebody has to have a totally clean, neat house, it's almost like a museum, then you're not as comfortable. You can see what their priorities are. Like I see mine as halfway decorated. You can see I don't spend my whole living, my life, decorating it. Like next door, you can see she has three kids. She doesn't have it totally decorated. It's nice; her house is kind of like mine. She tries to clean it. But you can tell kids live in it."

In essence, one must be clean, but not seem compulsive and overly self-conscious about the house. On the level of the house, cleanliness and order are also symbolic barriers to the chaos and uncertainty that threaten life in the garden. Being clean is the most important proof of moral worth. In Carolyn Kay Steedman's biography of her working-class mother in 1950s London, she writes evocatively about the class-bound significance of cleanliness. "I found a reference written by the local doctor for my mother who, around 1930, applied for a job as a ward-maid at the local asylum, confirming that she was clean, strong, honest, and intelligent. I wept over that, of course, for a world where some people might doubt her—my—cleanliness. I didn't care much about honesty, and I knew I was strong; but there are people everywhere waiting for you to slip up, to show signs of dirtiness and stupidity, so that they can send you back where you belong."[14]

CLASS, HOME, AND PLACE

Beltwayites' social location influences the cultural materials they use to make sense of the world. Their working-class status gives them a unique vantage point from which to look out on the rest of the world. This social position creates boundaries and parameters in which to act. In this sense, the culture of the last garden can be understood as a distinctively working-class phenomenon. The residents of Beltway use the visual landscape—in this case household display—to form and be transformed by the last garden. Given the power of the notion of Beltway as "the last stand" and the accurate (although racist)conviction that Beltway represents a way of life in danger of extinction, devout believers in place self-consciously manage the appearance of their homes to ward off the forces of decay and disorder. When people falter in their efforts to maintain the landscape—on the level of their homes—this is the first symptom that the promise of the last garden may be slipping away. Houseproud displays also magically strengthen Beltway's working-class inhabitants' tenuous grip on the American Dream. Neighbors anxiously guard Beltway by peering over fences and looking into windows to make mental notes about which neighbors are "taking care of things." Being clean establishes moral worth. Beltwayites cling so desperately to their ordered world because they cannot afford to take it for granted. For the middle and upper classes social ills and moral failings such as drug and alcohol abuse, domestic violence, teenage pregnancy, and poverty seem more distant, or at the very least are more carefully concealed. For the people of Beltway, the bungalows symbolize the attainment of a respectable life. Middle-class families give higher priority to ambition and happiness because respectability and decency are not particularly problematic for them. Beltwayites' veneration of property brings to life how the ordinary, mundane items that surround us affect and reflect who we are. Garden dwellers use the bungalows and lawns to craft the lived space— their place—of their social world. As working-class residents of the garden struggle to save money to purchase a home, and then work and talk ceaselessly about improving and protecting their homes, one wonders who owns what and what owns whom. Does owning a home transform people in Beltway or do Beltwayites transform the world around them through their homes?

When Carolyn Kay Steedman recalls her mother's life in working-class London, the values and the vantage points resonate with their counterparts in Chicago's Beltway half a century later. Steedman writes, "For my mother, who never got her house...the house was valuable in itself because of what it represented of the social world: a place of safety, wealth, and position, a closed door, a final resting-place. It was a real dream that dictated the pattern of our days. There are interpretations now that ask me to see the house my mother longed for as the place of undifferentiated, anonymous desire, to see it standing in her dream as the objects of fairy-tales do—princesses, golden geese, palaces—made desirable in the story simply because someone wants them."[15]

In these same fairy-tales, once the hero or heroine claims the prize of a princess, prince, palace, or golden goose, the story ends and the narrator promises us that the protagonists will live happily ever after. The people of Beltway are luckier than Steedman's mother, for they have gotten their wish. They have a house to call their own. But for the people of Beltway, the story does not end with a mortgage on a bungalow. Owning a bungalow only allows entry into the last garden: Creating and protecting the garden is a never-ending process requiring diligence and vigilance from all neighbors. Above all, the tidy rows of bungalows embody the order and abundance Beltwayites desire for themselves and their families. Safety, a sense of belonging, security, and undisrupted routines—these are the things neighbors want to preserve and these are the things they would mourn if the last garden ceased to exist.

•   •   •

Enthusiastic bungalow boosterism inspired by Chicago's recent Bungalow Initiative should not distract us from the fact that the recent efforts to retool and preserve the bungalow for the twenty-first century reflect growing concerns for the bungalows' (and the bungalows' owners') futures. A profound fragility defines life in the Bungalow Belt and working-class communities throughout the nation. It is fragility born of the social and economic precariousness of working-class life in a postindustrial age marked by workers' stagnant wages, deteriorating civic life, increased job insecurity, and longer work hours. The younger generation of Americans, for the first time in modern U.S. history, worries deeply about whether they will be able to be able to hold on to, much less exceed, the accomplishments of those who came before them. The chapter that follows builds on the notions of the bungalow and neighborhood—as evocative symbols of the garden's "cultivated order and abundance"—to extend the cultural significance of *place* to the level of the nation. Beltwayites' belief in America and the American Dream takes root in the ideals of home and community nurtured by garden living.

FOUR

For Country and Home

"THIS IS THE BEST COUNTRY IN THE WORLD"

When asked what they love about America, the people of Beltway answer, "Freedom, the freedom to do whatever you want." "This is the best country in the world." "There's no better place to live." "I couldn't live any place but America." "America to me is a blessing, I feel it is a blessing to live in this country." "America is the greatest place in the world." "There's no better place to live, right, or at least I don't know of any place." The core of their conviction is that America is a place where people are free, that is unencumbered by restrictions, to pursue the good life. In this view China and Cuba's tyrannies are not the result of dictatorships, ideology, or political philosophy; rather the failure of these political systems lies in the unwillingness of leaders to allow their citizens free rein to work and acquire for themselves and for their families. From this distinctively American perspective, freedom means freedom to care for one's family, to own a home, and to live in a place where one feels safe and comfortable.

The ideals of populism—respect for authority, mistrust of big government, and the defense of traditional morality—are at the core of how the working-class men and women of Beltway conceive of the nation. Midwestern populism tempered with the remnants of old world Catholicism leaves little room for liberalism despite working-class Chicagoans' historical ties to organized labor. As Jonathan Rieder writes about the Canarsie neighborhood in Brooklyn, "A distinctive politics of space" formed about the realities of home life, neighborhood life, and the "good life."[1] The values of respect for family, sacrifice, and hard work take form in the local and intimate places working-class Americans inhabit: humble neighborhoods, corner bars, VFW posts, and tidy kitchens. These values also represent the ideals that characterize a class-structured and place-bound understanding of the American way of life.

A sense of entitlement about "the last garden's" lifestyle serves "as a symbolic weapon against the nation's internal enemies"—enemies like the undeserving poor, welfare queens, gays, immigrants, and racial and ethnic minorities. As Rieder observes, "such resentments diminish hard-working, decent Americans by submerging their more generous impulses."[2] Liberals and other chroniclers of working-class politics of resentment may simplistically reduce this anger to racism and ignorance. But politicians regularly gain prominence and win reelection by pouring gasoline on incendiary social anxieties. By leading the charge against the marginalized members of society, political leaders transform minority interests into scapegoats for what is wrong with America. Beltway's inhabitants hold up their own respectability as evidence for why they are America's most deserving citizens. People are not born American, in this logic; being an American is something a citizen must earn through conduct and diligence. The nation embodies the very character of good and respectable working men and women.

During the holy days of the civic religion, Veterans Day, Memorial Day, and the Fourth of July, the garden's residents ritualistically invoke

America through the enthusiastic display of the Stars and Stripes. Beltwayites do not limit themselves to flying flags; patriotic neighbors tie dozens of tiny red, white, and blue ribbons to the branches of bushes and trees. The front of the house may be trimmed with red, white, and blue streamers, and signs in the front picture window wish passersby "Happy Fourth of July." Miniature flags are planted alongside the flowerbeds in the front and back garden. The country–style geese that adorn the front stoop and back garden get done up in Uncle Sam-inspired outfits. Huge sections of the neighborhood's visual landscape become part of this local celebration of America.

The streets and alleyway garages are lined with American-made cars. In Beltway, no one buys foreign cars and you would be hard pressed to find an auto shop that repairs foreign cars or stocks foreign parts. One time when I remarked on the difficulty of finding a part for my Toyota, a woman from the neighborhood chided me for not buying American.

The Beltway Civic League's motto declares "For country and home." The Civic League's insignia is a bald eagle holding two flags: the American flag and a flag with the letters "BCL." Underneath are the words, "Made up of residents interested in their community." Every Civic League meeting must start with the Pledge of Allegiance. As guardians of the neighborhood, the Civic League leadership takes responsibility for maintaining the flags that fly at the neighborhood's war memorial. When the flags need to be replaced, Civic League officers, aldermen, and local veterans gather at the memorial (a small brass plague and flag pole located on a small patch of lawn next to the bank parking lot). The group makes the event a time to remember the dead; local dignitaries lay a modest wreath of plastic flowers by the names of the fallen men as the new flags are raised.

The Beltway League's first meeting in September always begins the same way. Representatives from the offices of the aldermen, the city Clerk (a former West Ward alderman), the state representative, and the congressman make an appearance and pay their respects. President Ron Zalinsky, dressed in his nicest jacket and tie, exuberantly bangs his gavel to call the meeting to order. After welcoming everyone, he announces: "I want to thank the alderman for the POW/MIA flag, State Representative Lois McGee for the State of Illinois Flag, and Congressman Lipinski for the American flag." Flags are enormously important, explains the congressman. "Most people have a very keen understanding of what patriotism is. The American flag is enormously important to them because that is the flag soldiers went into battle under, that is the flag that many of their comrades died fighting for. I don't think you can have that intense patriotism unless you have people who have had that experience."

The ward's Democratic machine organization sponsors the annual Patriots' Day Parade for the Fourth of July. For the occasion, Archer Avenue is transformed into a mile-long river of red, white, and blue. From the little girls dressed up in their new red, white, and blue sundresses to the marchers made up to look like Uncle Sam or Lady Liberty, the annual Patriots' Day Parade is a day for everyone to celebrate Southwest Siders' particular vision of America. The parade has the usual marching bands and a seemingly endless supply of local politicians seeking office. Residents cynically note that it is always bigger and better during election years.

The parade also has a decidedly local, old-style, populist appeal, for it is open to anyone and everyone from the community who wishes to participate. Families line up along Archer Avenue and parents raise their children to their shoulders so youngsters can wave their toy flags at the marchers passing by. Groups ranging from area civic leagues to the Little League baseball teams to families from the neighborhood are welcome to march. Just decorate a car or bicycle with ribbons, balloons, and streamers and appear at Victory Park 45 minutes before the parade's starting time. Congressman Lipinski serves as the parade's understated master of ceremonies. Forgoing a vintage automobile to drive along the parade route, the congressman, casually dressed in his favorite White Sox baseball jacket, prefers to walk. He warmly greets voters and hands out candy to the local children. One local veteran remarks, "[The parades and services] get the community involved. People in the neighborhood really enjoy it. Like for the Fourth.... I can't believe all the people that come out there, waving and clapping, and they have the flags. It's just so enjoyable." Congressman Lipinski explains the history of the parade and his thinking in organizing the event for over two decades: "When I was first Alderman [in 1975], people had just moved to the area 15 years earlier and I don't think the area had much of a community identity. And I really started the Patriots' Parade for two reasons: one was to show the patriotism that existed in this community because patriotism at the time was under attack because of the situation in Vietnam. And two, to give the community a sense of identity and it brings people together."

The flags, the parades, and the sincere recitations of the Pledge of Allegiance at public meetings all serve to connect Beltwayites to their countrymen and their nation. On these occasions, the words "for country and home" come to life and the ties that bind the nation, community, and home become visible to all. Not only is the last garden the mythic place where inhabitants feel safe and comfortable and where homemakers struggle to make the good life possible; on the level of the nation, the last garden serves as a local outpost for American democracy.

THE VETERANS

Neighborhood Vietnam vets raise money by standing at busy intersections around the airport and selling POW/MIA flags to people stopped at traffic lights. One local vet who dutifully volunteers his time twice a year to collect money explains, "I go out there and do that because I work with the guys from Nam who are on waiting lists to get into VA hospitals. I go out there twice a year and sell those flags so that people can remember. I get so insulted when people only give me a buck. I mean, these guys went out there to fight for us back here. Whether or not the war was right or wrong, it doesn't matter. They went out there for us." In the words of the widow of a World War II veteran, "My husband died in World War II, my brother fought in Vietnam...they gave us freedom, freedom to do what we want, freedom of religion, freedom to go to school, freedom for everything. This is the best country in the world." A Vietnam veteran states: "America is the greatest country in the world. We've got our problems but every country out there does. [We soldiers] sacrificed what we did so that they could have what they have...new cars, their new homes...so they wouldn't have to live on the streets. People fought because they believed in this country and all that it means."

Defending America has less to do with noble sacrifice and more to do with the individual-level pursuit of happiness in the name of what America owes its people. These sentiments come through most dramatically when area veterans and their families talk about what these young men went off to war to defend. People are quite clear, if not defiant, about the fact that they were not fighting for politicians or ideologues, they were fighting for home and country. A Vietnam veteran insists, "I may have been naïve when I first enlisted, but ten seconds off the bus and I knew what I was getting into. This war, like every war, is about money, power.... But I was fighting for the people back home. I was fighting to come back for my life back here." These men were fighting for the promise of the good life for themselves and their families. They were fighting for the people back home in the neighborhoods and, most important, for the pursuit of happiness.

IMMIGRANTS AND FOREIGNERS: TAKING CARE OF OUR OWN

Given all the problems that exist at home, say many residents of Beltway, American policymakers should return to a policy of isolationism and concern themselves first and foremost with our people and our problems. America first is the battle cry. Beltwayites cheered on laws such as California's Proposition 187, which called for the elimination of some health and social services, including access to public education, for illegal aliens and their children.[3]

Even though many Beltway residents are the children and grandchildren of European immigrants, second- or third-generation Americans demonstrate little empathy for the latest wave of arrivals from Eastern Europe to settle in Chicago. Indeed, residents worry about how the local public schools' kindergarten programs are filled to capacity with children needing ESL instruction in Polish. They express outrage at new Poles who demand Polish-language masses. Neighbors complain that local "Polish" teenagers have formed gangs and are at the center of violence in the schools.[4] This animosity toward white, European immigrants is particularly striking given that Beltway has a large Polish-American population.[5] Ironically, Americanized Beltwayites will invoke their "Polish" heritage to justify their views on recent immigrants. In the words of one resident of Polish extraction, "I don't mind people moving in…the Spanish and the Poles. But why do they have to change the way we do things here? They should try to fit in. They should only speak English, and like the Poles and the Spanish have these different things they like to do at church. But why should we, I, have to change the way we have done things around here?"

First and foremost, Beltwayites see themselves as Americans. Being American symbolizes some level of success and achievement. Congressman Lipinski notes: "For the people here it is extremely important to their parents or their grandparents that they learn English so they really could be American citizens, and for the most part people here, the only way you could be a real and true American citizen is to have command of the English language." Hardworking, taxpaying American citizens insist that immigrants who have contributed nothing to this country cannot possibly be entitled to transfer payments and benefits from government relief programs.

Beltwayites speak harshly of foreigners who never make an effort to learn the language. Residents will yell at strangers in the street or a store and demand that they speak English. In the words of one woman, "Why should they get it easier than my parents? My grandparents had to learn English, nobody translated the forms for them. There was no welfare or health care. They were poor and were discriminated against. I don't have any problem with somebody getting help, but then everybody should get that help. Why should one group have it better than the next person?" She continues, "It's fine to have things in different languages, but then I think it's only fair to have everything in every language.... It just can't be in Spanish. Make it fair. Make it equal, have Polish, Spanish, Russian, Arabic, everything." A letter from a Beltway resident appeared in the March 7, 1996, edition of the *Southwest News Herald*. The letter, which was published under the headline "Immigrants Getting More Benefits Than Us," captures Beltwayites' resentment toward foreigners.

> Americans born and raised here better wake up! You have been the people paying the taxes all your life in this country. Too bad many of you or most of you are not entitled to the same benefits as many immigrants who never pay a dime in taxes.
>
> If they accept benefits from our country, they should start respecting it, mostly by speaking the English language. I feel it's an insult to the American people born here that a foreigner speaks in a foreign tongue in public. Talk at home if you want to, but in public, keep it in English.
>
> Secondly, I am sure that our retired Americans on fixed incomes could use food stamps and medical aid but since they are born here, they can't get this help. Americans born here should be equal to the same rights and benefits as foreigners. It seems as if Americans are losing control over their country. Thirdly, the foreigners don't seem to have respect for our laws or the American people.
>
> So, wake up America. Charity begins at home. Let's start helping Americans and our own people first.

The view that immigrants should make an effort to speak English is so widespread that Beltway's Congressman Lipinski has sponsored legislation to make English the official language of the United States. Area residents have given the plan their enthusiastic approval even though legal experts may question the proposed legislation's constitutionality. The government's effort to provide services for non–English speakers is viewed as more than a waste of tax money. To Beltwayites, refusing to use English is downright disrespectful and the government's policies, by tolerating such conduct, smack of favoritism and preferential treatment. It is an honor to live in the greatest country on Earth; every citizen ought to make the utmost effort to show his or her gratitude and loyalty by learning "our" language.

PATRONAGE, POLITICIANS, AND PAYING TAXES

During campaign season, lawns become the stage for street-level democracy in its purest form. Under the direction of—or in defiant opposition to—the local precinct captains, residents place massive campaign signs in the front yards in support of their candidate of choice. It is not unusual to see 15 to 20 signs—usually for the local machine candidates—along one block. Beltwayites depend on the patronage system that provides unionized city jobs, and upon retirement the state supplements their savings through pensions, Social Security, and other kinds of transfer payments.

Within machine politics, the responsibilities of citizenship are cast within a quid pro quo system. City workers dependent on the cronyism and tutelage of the powerful machines feel obligated to serve the ward as precinct captains or take a day off to work for a candidate on Election Day. City employees within machine-controlled wards believe that if they do not get out the vote "for their man" or for the union, their jobs and their benefits may be in jeopardy. Even those residents not employed by the city feel compelled to vote for the machine candidates because "if I don't the streets won't be cleaned, the trash won't be collected, the snow won't be plowed, and if I need something they won't get to me." Even if one does not work for the city, not voting gets one's neighbor the precinct captain in trouble. In a very real sense, a friend's job depends on "getting out the vote."

Flag-waving occasions provide elected officials with the opportunity to remind the citizenry of all the little things "the city that works" gives to its people. Remember that the machine makes sure that the streets are cleaned, the snow is plowed, and the trash is collected. During these events, we are reminded of what we Americans have achieved and hope to achieve. These are times to reinforce the ties that bind us together as a national community. Former Alderman John Puchinski explains, "The Beltway community is in the West Ward. There's 55,000 people in that ward. On a good election you might get 35,000 people coming out to vote. It'll take a lot of younger people to move in before that changes out there." He goes on, "On the North Side or in the lakefront wards, they're more liberal and people move in and out of apartment buildings and stuff. Here you have bungalows and people are here for a long time. Change as far as political change will come much slower here than in other areas." Puchinski details how the machine takes care of its own. "Chicago politics is unique. People were brought up so that the precinct captain comes to the door, and you tell the precinct captain you want the tree cut down, or you get your light fixed faster, get a new garbage can, help you out with jury duty, your kid needs a summer job… people will come and ask for help. That's just typical, long-standing Chicago politics. That's been the tradition of Democratic politics and there are still very strong wards left in the city of Chicago, and they are still strong in this area. So people tend to go to politicians or ward organizations for help. In turn, if someone helps you, what better way to support them but to come out and vote for them."

Not everyone is happy with the machine. While many residents accept it as part of a flawed system that grinds on to provide taxpayers with various amenities, other residents charge that the machine is a parasite feeding on apathy and patriotic loyalty. "The flag waving and patriotism, that's how they keep the machine going," argues Lillian Crimmins. Regardless, Beltwayites' loyalty to the nation persists. Lillian explains,

"The politicians use patriotism for their own purposes. But people are proud of this country. These are the people that go out and have died for America."

One might think Beltwayites' reliance on the state and public goods might lead people to have a more sympathetic view of the welfare state. Yet, as historians and other scholars have noted, the conservatism of America's working people leads them to reject a social democracy in order to vote for officials whose policies favor laissez-faire economics and corporate interests.

Beltwayites' opposition to transfer payments and the welfare system starts from working-class America's concerns and interests as taxpayers. Over and over again, Beltwayites invoke their status as taxpayers to explain their outrage at politicians, the government, the poor, foreigners, queers, criminals, blacks— the list goes on and on and varies at particular moments in history. As taxpayers, Beltway's inhabitants claim moral authority to vilify marginalized groups as scapegoats for America's woes. The rhetoric of resentment and entitlement takes shape in Beltwayites' economic insecurity and is echoed by talk radio and populist neoconservative voices like Ross Perot and Pat Buchanan. Taxes and excessive government spending epitomize the extravagant waste that violates the mores of decent, respectable citizens. A commonsense folk wisdom seems to inform residents' knee-jerk opposition to taxes of all kinds: politicians are corrupt and not to be trusted. Embracing values such as industriousness, living within one's means, proprietorship, and taking pride in the ownership of things would enable the government to serve its citizenry. The government could finally embody the values of the idealized notion of America.

The often told tales (from talk radio, the *Chicago Sun-Times,* and personal anecdotes) of waste, inefficiency, and indolence become parables instructing working people about the contradictions in their lives. Storytelling is an important means for reinforcing these ideological beliefs about America. Tales of welfare queens and Oval Office scandals prove what Beltwayites already know, the system is hopelessly corrupt and we deserving citizens must fight to get what we are entitled to claim as hard-working, employed, law-abiding, taxpaying citizens. Beltwayites particularly enjoy David and Goliath–like tales where the underdog goes up against the evil giant. Armed only with the slingshot of "people power," Beltwayites cast themselves as the courageous young hero who wins the battle for the side of righteousness.

PEOPLE POWER

In a recent Beltway Civic League bulletin, Helen Trevino, the bulletin's editor, wrote, "We need more taxes like a hole in the head." Alderman Puchinski became a hero in local lore when he defied Mayor Daley and Congressman Lipinski to vote against a proposed city tax hike. Puchinski had been Lipinski's political protégé for years, and the West Ward's machine organization maintains strong ties to Mayor Daley. The alderman's act of defiance led to his exile from the offices he had long shared with the congressman and to the status of persona non grata within the organization. The personal and professional rift between the two men continues to this day. But by his constituents in the neighborhood, Puchinski was hailed as a modern-day Robin Hood.

Most recently, Alderman Romanoski grabbed headlines when he claimed that the city's snow removal plan was yet another example of wasteful government spending. A politician who criticizes how "the city that works" gets things done is in grave danger of antagonizing a powerful mayor. But, in an interesting and telling twist of events, Alderman Stanley "Romi" Romanoski led a charge against the Department of Streets and Sanitation and the mayor.

Chicago is a city where snow can make or break a career. Just ask Michael Bilandic and Jane Byrne.[6] Romi found himself going head to head with Daley when the Southwest Side alderman charged that the city had gone overboard about the threat of snow one weekend, needlessly draining the city treasury of hundreds of thousands of dollars. Romanoski told a *Chicago Tribune* reporter that Streets and Sanitation "had trucks out all Friday night into Saturday morning and Sunday morning for close to 10 hours, but I didn't get enough snow on my windshield to turn my wipers on." Announcing that he planned to submit a Freedom of Information request to get to the bottom of the matter, the alderman declared, "Somebody has to explain what the criteria are for a full alert and why it cost the taxpayers $1 million for an inch of snow." He claimed that at times during the weekend, Streets and Sanitation had a full complement of 240 trucks out. Ironically, Romanoski based his strong criticism on his 20-year career with Streets and Sanitation, along with complaints from West Ward residents who "saw a lot of plows out there with nothing to do." The press found the alderman's comments surprising, the mayor fumed to reporters, and the commissioner of Streets and Sanitation went so far as to call her former colleague "a nitwit." Romanoski had hoped his bold words would help win the respect of Southwest Side voters. To outsiders, his political grandstanding seemed reckless and ill conceived. But back home in Beltway, the alderman understood that whistle blowing on any kind of government waste, even waste in the name of improved city services, would resonate with voters. Beltwayites' fiscally conservative, no-nonsense, common-sense approach to the world makes the idea of spending city revenues "on a lot of plows with nothing to do" as wasteful as throwing money out the window.

Another story that brings to life Beltway activists' ongoing battles for the betterment of ordinary citizens is the fight over neighborhood ambulance service. Stan Marino, a retired machine operator, is a stout bald man in his late sixties or seventies whose round, jovial appearance belies his argumentative nature. He has lived in the neighborhood his entire life. Stan has long been active in neighborhood politics and is on a first-name basis with every local politician. Over the past several years he has been an outspoken member of the BCL and the ward zoning board. Like many local activists, he views himself as a watchdog for the neighborhood. When a friend and neighbor approached Stan about the gerrymandered boundaries for ambulance service, the longtime activist enthusiastically took on the cause.

In case of emergencies, residents from the eastern part of the neighborhood are taken to a neighborhood hospital, St. Elizabeth's, and residents from the western section go to the Lourdes hospital. The hospitals are nearly equidistant from the neighborhood. In Stan's tale, an elderly resident of the community falls ill. The man's regular physician is at Lourdes, but the man lives in the section of the neighborhood assigned to St. Elizabeth's. Despite the man and his wife's insistent pleas that he be taken to Lourdes, the man eventually goes to St. Elizabeth's, but later the same day he is transferred to Lourdes where his regular cardiologist can supervise his treatment for the remainder of his hospital stay.

To residents, the story of the ambulance is yet another example of how big government and bureaucracy hurt ordinary people in their everyday lives. "Why can't a man go to the hospital he wants!" demands Stan. "Our tax dollars pay for the paramedics and the ambulances, they should do what we say." As Stan recounts the story of his friend once again, he pounds his fist on the table and the other BCL members nod their heads and talk among themselves about the terrible waste and stupidity of such a policy. One woman cries out, "Maybe I should drag myself west over the railway tracks while I'm having a stroke so I can get to my hospital." Stan regularly tells the story at community meetings, and the local newspaper has reported on the situation several times. BCL members never seem to tire of hearing the tale.

Several months after Stan first raised the matter at the monthly Civic League meeting, the community relations aide from the congressman's office came to address residents' complaints about the situation. The aide, Jim Lisowski, calmly explained to BCL members that Medicare would cover the cost of the ambulance transfer. He repeatedly assured residents that they would have no out-of-pocket expenses if they needed to be transferred from one hospital to another for a longer stay. "Medicare will completely cover the costs, 100 percent, if you have a problem simply call my office," the young aide calmly answered the crowd. Stan shook his head and waved his hands as if he were scolding his grandson: "Oh no, no, no...but it's wasting money, why won't you take us where we want?" The congressman's aide still looked puzzled. "But you don't have to pay, Medicare covers everything." Stan shot back, "It's our money, you're still wasting our money." "But it's tax money, you don't pay anything," the aide said again, in a tone that indicated to Stan and the others that the younger man still did not understand their point of view. Stan yelled back, " Medicare, it's still my money. It comes out of my pocket." Even though Medicare covers the costs, the Civic League's old-timers experienced the policy as wasteful government slyly slipping the money out of their pockets.

These anecdotes illustrate how taxpayers' proprietorship and ownership of America and its resources obfuscate a more communitarian vision of America. In Beltway, much civic engagement takes shape as individuals come together to look out for what America owes us. When Beltwayites—especially those over 65—see their health care not delivered efficiently or Social Security under threat, they respond with a loud, unmistakable fury. To residents, these government transfer payments represent possessions they own, just like the car in their driveway or the tidy little bungalow. Beltwayites believe a lifetime of paying taxes has earned them an IOU from politicians and the government.

NATIONALISM AND PATRIOTISM IN EVERYDAY LIFE

In Beltway, the Pledge of Allegiance starts everything from Civic League meetings, local school council sessions, and VFW gatherings, to Bingo and homeroom. During the Leahy Park summer camp program, the youngsters begin each day with the Pledge. The youngest group of children, aged three and four, cannot quite manage the words to the complete Pledge, so they recite a shorter poem called "My Flag." Each morning the children fight among themselves over who gets to hold the tiny flag Ms. Martin has for the daily ritual. Neely Martin, the head of the park day camp program, says: "Saying the Pledge of Allegiance, it instills values. That value that this is your country. It would be nice if the kids could learn respect for something. It's just a tradition, what they grew up with and they do because of honor to the flag and country." When the Civic League membership celebrated the group's thirty-fifth anniversary, a dinner was held in the banquet room of a local restaurant. As Ron called on everyone to rise for the Pledge, he noticed there was no flag in the room. For a moment, there was confusion; then the officers instructed the gathering to turn to the left and recite the Pledge to a flag that was not there.[7]

Beltwayites' devotion to the flag grows out of the belief in the flag as a symbol for what is best about America. The belief in the patriotic and nationalistic ideals of America is also reflected in residents' devoted admiration for veterans and the armed services. The Beltway Civic League's monthly newsletter arrives in a envelope with a stamped message commemorating POWs and MIAs. For the past several years, one of the BCL's pet projects has been a letter-writing campaign to promote the issuing of a stamp in remembrance of POWs and MIAs. As the neighborhood's primary public building, the Beltway branch of the Chicago Public Library is an integral part of civic life. For several months Lydia Donovan, the head branch librarian, allowed local veterans to display memorabilia from their military service. The most striking part of the exhibit featured a GI Joe doll made up to look like a POW being tortured in a replica of a bamboo cage constructed out of toothpicks. BCL members and local residents who had worked so tirelessly to build the library facility and who were so proud of their beautiful new building felt that it would be the natural location for a larger memorial commemorating residents' military duty.

Military service remains an esteemed path among young men and women in the neighborhood. The *Southwest News Herald* features a regular column titled "Military Notes" announcing area residents' promotions and assignments. Many of Beltway's older residents served in

World War II or the Korean conflict, and many of them gladly and proudly sent their sons off to Southeast Asia during the 1960s and early '70s. A number of Beltwayites now in their forties went off to serve in Southeast Asia after graduating from high school. Almost every Beltway resident has a close friend or family member who fought in Vietnam. Many Beltwayites know young men who never came back or who were so scarred and traumatized by their experiences overseas that they were left physically and psychologically incapacitated.

It is the area veterans who organize programs for children at local schools, raise money for poor and ill veterans, and ride in the annual parades in cars decorated with flags and homemade signs for the local VFW. Now that they have returned home to their local communities, these men serve as the guardians of America and the American way of life. For instance, in the campaign literature for the 1995 aldermanic election, two of the six candidates made prominent mention of their military service as proof of their suitability for office. Local politicians, activists, and community leaders will also invoke their military experience during public meetings to claim authority for the ideals of community life and in a larger sense their vision of America. It is as if having fought for your country adds weight to your words. During a community meeting to speak with candidates, one aldermanic candidate called on the neighbors to "keep the integrity of our neighborhoods, and our American way of life. The answer lies in the past, the principles and morals that we had, we have to bring them back.... I am a U.S. Army veteran, so I have the experience and ideas to be alderman."

"The distance Middle America feels from the country and the doubts it has about the government and its leaders contrast sharply with the close supportive feelings it appears to have for the nation," writes Herbert Gans. "People feel loyalty to the nation because it is something more than Big Government, the country, or an entity that controls domestic politics."[8] In the words of one longtime resident, "The nation is where you live. It's part of you. It gives you a bond with everybody else that is part of your country. We're together." The nation itself is a symbol.

As with their Catholicism, the working-class people of Beltway are indoctrinated in the rituals of patriotism at an early age.[9] "In contemporary society, the nation-state has become a norm and nationality, a commonsense frame of reference. Nationality is one of those conceptions—like gender—which lies unacknowledged (most of the time) behind many of our everyday actions and structures what is thought."[10] Beltwayites proudly fly their flags for national holidays and march down the streets of the neighborhood to honor and remember those who have given their lives for America and its proud way of life. American national identity flavors everyday life in familiar ways, and this seemingly natural rhetoric of nationality serves as an unnoticed backdrop for civic life.

Although the nation may officially be represented by the makers of foreign policy, "judging by the polls, people appear to treat it as an abstract and expressive symbol to be identified with rather than to be used for debating foreign policy."[11] The nation is actually a symbol that Americans can adapt to their own purposes, and yet people, all the while, do not believe they owe the nation anything more than the taxes they pay. There is a cynicism toward the country, the government, America's economic dominance, politics, and politicians, but at the end of the litany of complaints and criticisms, Beltway's working-class residents will always insist that "I love America." To Kathy Fenton, "Because of what America stands for, that's why they like to say they're Americans. Total freedom, wealth, opportunity . . . those are the things that I grew up reading in my history books. But I think the majority of people, I mean the wealth stays among 20 percent of the people and 80 percent of the people share 20 percent of the money. But that doesn't mean I don't love it."

The Beltway Civic League's motto, "For country and home," dramatically demonstrates the link among local place, local politics, and a symbolic collective ideal of our nation. Taking care of your family, home, and community is the same as being a good citizen. Former Beltway Civic League President Robert Sherman, a firefighter and veteran, wrote about his thoughts on citizenship in an essay he titled "Civics." The essay, written in the 1960s, outlines the connection between nation and family and warns neighbors that failure to participate in local community life undermines democracy and leaves the door open for oppression and autocracy. When Sherman compares citizenship to parenthood, he suggests that too many people are citizens without understanding the full moral gravity of the job.

"CIVICS"

A word that embodies an attitude for which many people shrug their shoulders and assume that they are not obligated to become active or a participant. This is an error that many people make [in many other countries] that have none of these rights, we will wager that these people who also became apathetic and lazy as so many Americans are becoming now would leap hastily to regain the right to become more active, voice their opinions, and shape their communities.

In actual truth, the most important jobs in the world are given to Amateurs—and they are citizenship and parenthood. Both of these are tough jobs and a proud parent and good citizen need never bow their heads to anyone.

In Beltway, there are few people who doubt that they are or should be part of the American nation. Beltwayites resist trends toward multiculturalism and labels such as Irish American, Polish American, or Mexican American. Despite the fact that many residents are first- or second-generation Americans who remember when English was not the only language spoken in their home, the unqualified American ethnicity is the one most residents enthusiastically embrace. Beltwayites describe themselves as American and correct you if you pronounce their names in a European way. "It's Salva-tor, not Salva-toray. I am an American." "It's Villareal, not Viya-ray-al. I am an American." "I hate those Affirmative Action forms, you know what I always do. I always write in 'American' and check that." "My people are part mick and polack but I'm American." The cultural dimensions of national identity, that is, the sets of meanings and values with which Beltwayites describe "our country" and "our way of life," serve as the symbolic elaboration of the sense of place on the level of the nation. Toni Capelevski insists, "Saying you're American distances yourself from your immigrant roots, the poverty people are trying to escape. Being able to say you're American means you have made it. People love America because it is better than where you came from." Being a flexible symbol, the nation serves further needs and wishes. It is a symbol of strength, supporting people's desire for security and insulating them from threats to their enjoyment of the good life. The success of America takes root in a uniquely American ideology that says that pursuing individual interest and the American dream is equivalent to being a good citizen. It is as if taking care of your family, your home, your community, and loving your country are the same acts. The family and the home are tied to this idealized (and imagined) symbol of America.

MOURNING AMERICA

No one remembers how long there has been a Memorial Day Parade in Beltway. Local veterans, ranging in ages from forties and fifties (for those who fought in Vietnam) to seventies (for those who fought in World War II), come out to remember and remind others of how ordinary men like themselves served their nation in times of crisis. The parade route takes marchers through the Beltway and Carver Heights neighborhoods. Men gather at the Minuteman Park field house early in the morning. Chicago's typically gray, drizzly, cold weather in May means that parade participants layer their brown, blue, and gray veterans' uniforms and caps with flannel jerseys and dark overcoats. Men carry the flags of the post, and a smattering of teenagers from the local public high school band arrive at the park ready to march. Most of the band members are African American and Hispanic kids, who, although quite polite and respectful, seem somewhat mystified by the old white men and their preparations. From year to year, elected officials such as the alderman or congressman may pay their respects to the gathering of veterans.

When it is not an election year, no one is surprised by the politicians' absence. Truth be told, no one seems to miss them.

Marchers joke among themselves about Chicago's harsh climate and boast that in years past snow and freezing wind chills could not stop their pilgrimage through the streets of the neighborhood. One man remarks, "I remember one year [for Veterans' Day] the icicles were forming on our faces, and we still went out to march." The others nod as they recall previous vigils. Another man asks, "Is this all that's coming?" His companion responds, "The cold weather kept them away." Shaking his head, "Nah, it's not that bad, now I've seen worse. One year people didn't come out because the downtown one was canceled, but we still were going. Ah, I've marched when it's much colder." As if to emphasize his point, the old man tightens his grip around the flag he holds. Many of the older men have come to participate, but instead of walking the parade route, they opt to drive American-made cars decorated with homemade signs and tiny flags. Dave, a Vietnam veteran in his forties, serves as the parade marshal. When Dave calls the marchers to attention, a solemn quiet falls over the gathering as they begin to arrange themselves in uneven rows of four or five. Dave runs ahead to conduct traffic to make sure that on-coming cars wait. Joe, a Korean War veteran in his sixties riding a gold-colored cruising bike, goes out front first to lead the way. The parade is officially under way when Joe eases his gigantic bike out of the driveway. A tape of military music is blaring on the motorcycle's tape deck. Men holding flags and banners follow behind the motorcycle, then come a dozen or so members of the high school marching band, followed by a convoy of Buicks, Fords, and Chryslers. A small number of women participate in the parade as members of the Ladies Auxiliary. It is early in the morning on a cold, rainy spring day, and so there are not many people on the streets. A few passersby have stopped. On the sidewalk a father kneels down beside his son to explain what the procession means and what the men are doing.

The marchers make their way down Taylor Avenue, the busiest commercial artery along the boundary between Carver Heights and Beltway, to the final destination, the Reynolds Funeral Home parking lot. Jack Reynolds has long since passed on, and his son now runs the family business. Jack himself served in the military, and he first offered his parking lot to area veterans so long ago that nobody recollects performing the Memorial Day ceremony anyplace else. In neighborhoods like Beltway, funeral home directors are respected members of the community and local residents appreciate the Reynolds family's generosity. The cars and trucks in the procession wind their way through the parking lot and park off to the side while the men and women carrying flags solemnly proceed to the far end of the lot beside the funeral home. Members of the Ladies Auxiliary run in and out of the funeral home back door carrying ice chests filled with cans of soda and food. The food is spread out on long folding tables underneath a small tent. Post Commander Casimir "Cas" Kuchera, a distinguished-looking man in his seventies wearing a long overcoat over his neatly pressed brown uniform, announces that there will be free hot dogs and "pop" for all the ceremony participants and well-wishers who have gathered in the parking lot. He stands at the back edge of the rain-soaked parking lot pointing and barking orders at all the men as they assemble the sacred shrine for the memorial service.

The chaplain, commander-in-chief, senior vice commander-in-chief, junior vice commander-in-chief, and chaplain of the Ladies Auxiliary stand on the walkway beside the parking lot and funeral home. The chaplain turns on the small portable microphone and asks everyone to approach the shrine because "we want to get started." VFW memorial services throughout the United States follow a ritual established by the national organization of the Veterans of Foreign Wars and the Ladies Auxiliaries. But while the text has a set format, each VFW post adapts the service to meet the needs of the local membership. In Beltway, because there is no permanent shrine to veterans, the local post constructs a temporary one for these rites. Indeed, the most striking and evocative element of the memorial ceremony is the shrine itself. A rectangular piece of plastic green turf, the size of a grave, is carefully laid out on the parking lot tarmac. At the head of the grave is a white wooden cross.

During the service, post members circle around the grave and the color guard stands at attention holding their flags and banners.

The memorial ritual itself, which is infused with religious and nationalist themes and images, symbolizes a kind of communion of the civic religion. At one point in the service, Christ is referred to as "the Captain of Our Salvation." In fact, the ritual's use of the reader-and-response format evokes a typical Christian church service. The responses read by the commanders-in-chief and Ladies Auxiliary chaplain come directly from the Bible. It is the post chaplain who officiates at the rite. Below is the text of the service.

CHAPLAIN:	Comrade Commander-in-Chief, to whom should the true soldier look for help in the battles of life?
COMMANDER-IN-CHIEF:	"Our help is in the name of the Lord, who made heaven and earth."
CHAPLAIN:	Comrade Senior Vice Commander-in-Chief, what assurance have we of a prolonged stay among the scenes and activities of earth?
SENIOR VICE COMMANDER-IN-CHIEF:	"For we are strangers before Thee, and sojourners, as were all our fathers; our days on earth are a shadow, and there is none abiding."
CHAPLAIN:	Comrade Junior Vice Commander-in-Chief, have you a message of condolence for those bereaved?
JUNIOR VICE COMMANDER-IN-CHIEF:	I have. The Book of Life tells us that "Like as a father pitieth his children, so the Lord pitieth them that fear Him. For he knoweth our fate; he remembereth that we are dust."
CHAPLAIN:	What message has the Chaplain of the Ladies Auxiliary?

CHAPLAIN OF THE LADIES AUXILIARY: I have a message of hope that should inspire our comrades at this solemn moment and all through life. The message is from the Captain of Our Salvation. He says: "I am the resurrection and the life; he that believeth in me, though he were dead, yet shall he live; and whosoever liveth and believeth in me shall never die."

CHAPLAIN: Comrades, we are thankful for these inspiring thoughts. Let us learn the lesson of the hour which is that we too are nearing the end of life's pilgrimage and sooner or later these services may be held in our memory.

Let us live that when our summons comes we may depart with a good conscience, in the comfort of sincere religion, belief in God, and perfect charity toward all mankind. Let us pray.

At this point, departed soldiers are commemorated with symbolic tributes to the shrine. After the chaplain says the words, "Comrades, in commemorating the virtues of our departed heroes who served their country in time of need we now offer our symbolic tributes," he places flowers on the grave with the words "These red flowers symbolize the zeal of our departed comrades in upholding brotherhood, truth, and justice." The post commander-in-chief makes the same offering, this time with white flowers, which are a "token of the purity of affection we have for our departed comrades." Then the present commander-in-chief places blue flowers upon "this sacred shrine" as he recites the words: "The blue of our national standard symbolizes truth and fidelity. Therefore I place these blue flowers from nature's bosom in token of our sincere respect for all departed comrades." Finally the Ladies Auxiliary president places an evergreen wreath on the sacred shrine with the words "This wreath is a symbol of eternity. Its color bespeaks life everlasting. Thus do we say that the deeds of our soldiers, sailors, airmen, and marines, on land, on sea, and in the air, are immortalized in the hearts of a grateful people." The post commander then reads off the names of post members who have died in the past year, and the chaplain asks everyone to sing "America." The chaplain gives another benediction and there is a closing prayer. The service concludes with the marching band's best trumpeter playing Taps. Post members then use the fire escape to climb to the roof of the funeral parlor to fire a gun salute. The grave remains on the tarmac for several more minutes, and family members stand beside the shrine, heads bowed and eyes closed in silent prayer. Widows, children, and grandchildren may leave flowers on the grave. After people have had their time at the shrine, the VFW members roll up the flags, fold the green turf, and dismantle the cross. The flowers and wreath are plastic so everything is just stored away to be used again next year.

I asked one woman, a family member of a soldier who had fought and died in Southeast Asia, why the ceremony was performed in the parking lot. She stated matter-of-factly, "This is the way it's always been done." I questioned, "But why not a permanent memorial or a cemetery?" Looking me straight in the eye, she spoke simply but insistently: "But we have to do it *here*." *Here* means the neighborhood—this local place—the ceremony must take place for our fallen brothers from the neighborhood. The woman continued, "The ceremony is not for anybody else. It's for our people. Of course it's gotta happen here." The Memorial Day ceremony captures the essence of the meaning of "nation" for Beltway residents. One of the central elements of the ceremony is the veneration of the nation. It is as if the very ritual itself brings America to life on the local level, and, if only for a moment, nation, neighborhood, and home intersect on a single symbolic plane.

The ongoing dialogue between larger societal structures (the media, politicians, the state) and actors on the local level is what brings America, the nation, to life. The imaginings, that is, the symbolic work and rituals surrounding patriotism and nationalism—the flags, the memorials, the children dressed in red, white, and blue, and of course the parades—are the neighborhood-level rituals and symbols of the imagined community that is America. As a cultural event, these civic events generate the collective effervescence that allows Beltway's garden dwellers to construct America, the nation, and then, more specifically, to imagine a vision of America which resonates with their own values and morality. In a fundamental sense, America lives in the neighborhood.

Let us consider the imagined America Beltwayites have created. On one level, Beltwayites' national pride—and perhaps even patriotism—simply means the individual-level pursuit of the American Dream. In effect, one can love the nation because it justifies the pursuit of the good life. According to Kathy Fenton, "Listening to my grandfather who served in World War II and my uncle who served in Vietnam…everybody that's come from somewhere else has the idea that they're gonna come here and that's gonna make things easier for them. That they're going to be extremely rich, they're gonna live in big, beautiful houses, and it's a wonderful country to live in."

On another level, patriotism and the nation foster a sense of essential solidarity and community. The nation provides support because, at the end of the day, we know we belong to something magical and greater than ourselves. Something of the nature of the "passionate patriotism—this political love—citizens feel for the nation can be deciphered from the ways in which languages describe its object: either in the vocabulary of kinship (motherland, *Vaterland, patria*) or that of home."[12] Both images denote something to which one is naturally tied.

Literary historian Benedict Anderson writes, "In this way, nationness is similar to skin color, gender, and parentage—all those things one cannot help. And in these natural ties, one senses what one might call the 'beauty of *gemeinshchaft*.' To put it another way, precisely because such ties are not chosen, they have about them a halo of disinterestedness. The family has traditionally been conceived as the domain of disinterested love and solidarity. So too, although historians, diplomats, politicians, and social scientists are quite at ease with the idea of national interest, for most ordinary people of whatever class the whole point of the nation is that it is interestless. Just for that reason, it can ask for sacrifices."[13]

These nested relationships between family/neighborhood and neighborhood/nation demonstrate the process by which national identity is simply a reconceptualization of a microlevel local culture on the level of a macrolevel national identity and culture. The Beltway Civic League illustrates this connection in its motto, "For country and home." Defending home, neighborhood, and nation—it is as if these three apparently separate entities have a trinitarian relationship, simultaneously distinct yet unitary. Protecting America translates into protecting a way of life that exists within the neighborhoods and within the home.

A recent BCL newsletter headline proclaimed "New Flags are Flying." The story reads:

> Alderman Stan Romanoski, John Hunt, an aide for Congressman Lipinski, and State Representative Mary Kelly and the BCL officers dedicated two new flags at the Veterans Memorial at Third and Iroquois. . . . If you had been there, you would have heard our proud Alderman mention to Civic League officers that the fence at the memorial was in bad condition and that he would see to it that the fence will be redone. Thank you Alderman Romanoski.

BCL officers praise the alderman for revering the connection between nation and home, nation and neighborhood. Residents are "proud" to hear that the alderman is outraged at the condition of the fence around the memorial. The objects from the neighborhood and local life constitute the stuff of the nation. As imagined entities, America and Americanness live only because of the veterans' rituals, parades, flags, and heartfelt recitations of the Pledge.

And this connection between the nation and the local also provides the foundation for seeing the local community's problems as a microcosm of the problems that plague the nation as a whole. National-level discourse about crime, race, family, poverty, welfare, and young people initially takes shape in the school yards, corner pubs, backyards, churches, living rooms, and kitchens of places like Beltway. These everyday discussions about "the trouble with kids today," "those people on welfare," "families falling apart," "the new people coming into the neighborhood," and "keeping people safe in their own homes" become reworked as a national discourse about what it means to live in America and how we Americans can work to maintain this way of life. While one rejoices in how the local community serves as the basis for America's public policy debates and American values, these locally grown visions of the nation may also go some way to explaining myopic America First ideology.

In the process of constructing the American identity, being American becomes a kind of code word for working-class Beltwayites' claims to respectability. Discarding the label Polish, Irish, Italian, or Mexican means that you have made it; "Americanness" is a badge of honor in the pursuit of the American Dream. Moreover, by claiming an American identity, Beltwayites erect boundaries between themselves and others, the "others" they want to exclude from the rights and privileges inextricably tied to being American. Certain groups are seen as ineligible and undeserving (the poor, immigrants, etc.) because they do not pay taxes or have failed to recognize the last garden's moral order as a distinctively American system of values.

To the working men and women of Beltway, the nation is a revered symbol, particularly during national holidays. Although these occasions are commingled with leisure time activities and may have turned into retail sales events, these holidays are still devoted to the practice of the civic religion. As Commander Kuchera told a crowd of nearly 100 veterans and families gathered for Veterans Day services, "We are here today because we know today is more than sales at Montgomery Ward or Target."

Public officials and politicians celebrate the ideals of the nation to prove that despite what the public thinks of politicians, politics, and the government, we are all part of something bigger and better. Politicians use such holy days of the civic faith to remind local residents of all elected officials have done for them. Anderson observes, "With respect to national anthems, no matter how trite the words or mediocre the tunes, there is in this singing an experience of simultaneity. At precisely such moments, people wholly unknown to one another utter the same verses and sing the same melody."[14] Being patriotic and loving America seems so natural that it is no longer questioned.

Loving the nation is an organic part of Beltwayites' everyday lives just like the flags that fly on their bungalows and the big American-made cars that line the streets and alleyway garages. The flags, the cars, bumper stickers remembering POWs and MIAs or encouraging consumers to buy American, these are tangible expressions of residents' connection to America. "They hang flags to show unity as a country. They hang their flags to show that they're supportive of men that are fighting at war, that have fought in war.... People have a need to believe. Nobody wants to send their son into the war thinking they are doing it for nothing. They need to believe there is a reason behind it," declares Kathy Fenton. Grand visions for the nation's sense of place take root in the idyllic possibilities of the last garden; the imagining of America is done in tandem with the making of home and neighborhood. Being a good American, in the simplest and most basic terms, is the same as being a good neighbor and a good homemaker.

The Last Garden

A CAUTIONARY TALE IN DENIAL

Garden dwellers' fears seep into the experience of everyday life. Proving one's respectability requires the constant reinforcement of the moral boundaries that distinguish the deserving and undeserving, the good and bad neighbors, and the decent and the indecent. In this world, how you decorate your home, the American-made car in your back alley garage, and what the neighbors think of you serve as props in a class-based social performance that dramatizes your social worth. Within the mythic last garden, cultivating the appearance of order and abundance keeps the world from coming apart at the seams. It is not simply that bungalows have played an important historical and architectural role in the democraticization of homeownership. Rather, bungalows stand as monuments to hardworking men and women who embrace "American" values surrounding home, neighborhood, and nation. Without the idyllic promise of the last garden, there is no way to create meaning in everyday life, and without meaning, chaos threatens to overtake us.

At the start of the book, I ask the question: What is it that the people of Beltway would mourn the loss of if Beltway ceased to exist? The answer I offer is a *distinctive sense of place,* for places achieve significance because they can be the source of intense emotion. On the level of the home, household display and decoration reinforce women's claims to respectability through their social roles as wives, mothers, and homemakers. On the level of the neighborhood, a sense of place inspires civic engagement in response to assaults on the landscape in the form of graffiti and disorder. On the level of the nation, ideals about what it means to be American and the definition of the American Dream take shape in the local values that dictate the pattern of everyday life.

In the simplest terms, the most important lesson from Beltway is that denial and uncertainty permeate working-class life.[1] Some of things that Beltwayites deny include the thinness of the socioeconomic gap between themselves and the poor, the problems of crime, drugs, gangs, and violence lurking right at their door, and the uncertainty of their future claims to moral order and social stability. The community's trauma in the wake of the Powell and Harvey murders comes not so much from the tragic nature of the girls' deaths. Instead, the murders overwhelm the community because the circumstances surrounding the killings strike a mortal blow to the rules and expectations garden dwellers rely on to navigate the world. Over and over again, residents claim the murders would have made more sense, and local activists would have responded more cohesively, if the race and class backgrounds of the murderers had not violated residents' understandings of the destructive forces that threaten their way of life. After all, good kids from good homes are not supposed to steal a gun and start shooting at innocent people. In the garden, moral order is inscribed in the perfectly cleaned houses, manicured grass, graffiti-free streets, and the bumper stickers that remember POWs and MIAs. Beltwayites believe that if you study the garden, you can see the solid, respectable, working-class values celebrated in the visual appearance of place. Consumption patterns and the care and the display of material possessions serve as a bulwark to working-class residents' claims to social status and stability.

Beltway's proximity to the ghetto puts into relief the racial context of working-class fear; race is not the only source of the anxiety. White working-class Americans have always felt squeezed between the top and bottom, and poor blacks are just one of the targets for working-class resentments. It is too easy and simplistic to account for working-class white rage with racist belief systems. On the most fundamental level, physical proximity to the ghetto deeply troubles garden dwellers because it reminds them how close they are socially and economically to their less fortunate neighbors trapped in the ghetto. Beltwayites' racism then can be seen as a byproduct of their efforts to fortify the cultural and moral boundaries between themselves and more stigmatized groups. Class-bound ideologies and boundaries make it difficult for garden dwellers to reconcile themselves to existence of *white* teenage mothers, *white* homeless, *white* drug addicts, *white* gangbangers, *white* single mothers, and poor *whites*. Whites are respectable, and respectability keeps people safe from the dangers posed by destructive social forces. If Beltwayites' class-bound philosophy reveres hard work and individual sacrifice as the path to order and abundance, those who fall from grace (even with the garden's protection), prove beyond a shadow of a doubt that the world is spinning out of control. When people who "play by the rules" are not safe, then stability and security must be illusions. The veneer of respectability may not be attained and maintained.

Resentment toward welfare programs, immigrants, and taxes seems counterintuitive only from the liberal perspective. A more communitarian orientation calls for the expansion of benefits available to all. But it is easy to speak about social justice and equity from the perspective of the social and cultural elites. The privileged have little contact with and face almost no competition from upwardly mobile minorities looking for their piece of the pie.

Instead a uniquely working-class strategy for survival relies on creating social and symbolic distances between themselves and the dispossessed as the working class deny their own marginality. The politics of working-class resentment charges that disadvantaged groups manipulate and overstate the significance of racism, discrimination, poverty, unjust treatment under the law, and unequal law enforcement. In a striking and inconsistent blend of entitlement and self-congratulatory individualism, Beltwayites manage a delicate balance of believing in the power of self-interest and moral superiority, all the while insisting that the very same self-interest, individualism, and moral superiority earn them the right to use government programs when the need arises. It is almost as if they are saying, "I don't need anybody, just make sure you don't touch my Social Security, Medicare, and don't make me pay more taxes for the programs I have earned."

Creating a façade of moral worth and social status requires elaborate cultural, economic, and social effort. Beltwayites' anger and self-righteousness mask their insecurity about constantly being scrutinized and evaluated by the social world. In the words of one garden dweller who momentarily penetrates the self-consciousness of garden living, "It takes hard work to live this way." Residents' anxiety, denial, and ongoing efforts to keep up appearances grow out of the nagging fear that they cannot afford to make a mistake or else the entire world will come crashing down around them.

Beltwayites charge that affirmative action and welfare are unfair because "no one marched for my grandparents" when they worked in factories and lived in the tenements. In point of fact, the statement is false. Saul Alinsky, the CIO, and laborers themselves marched in the streets. Progressive and radical elements joined forces to demand justice for the Poles, Italians, Greeks, Jews, Irish, and Italians when nativist bigots questioned the ethnics' claims to whiteness, and thus respectability.

Such selective memory among today's working-class white ethnics may be the result of ignorance about one's history, but it also speaks to the seductive power of American individualism. Working-class whites were activists on the radical fringes when the need suited them, but after they had achieved a modicum of success, they did not look behind them and reach out a hand in solidarity to change the system that had oppressed them. When you have to keep up with mortgage payments, to put food on the table, and the America Dream's promise seems to lie just within your grasp, you no longer have time for revolution. Saul Alinsky's blue-collar revolutionaries abandoned the fight when racial integration threatened precious property values and racial identity. The ugly, vile racism that characterized blacks as morally deficient and subhuman fed off working-class whites' fears and insecurities about their *own* hold on social status. In a sense, Beltwayites' rage toward the ghetto seems like misdirected antipathy they mean to direct at the elite institutions and privileged people who sit at the top of the socioeconomic food chain. The possibility that the hardworking working classes might join the ranks of the powerful is what keeps the subordinated from turning on the "people above," who reap the greatest benefits from the system's inequality.

WHAT DOES THE FUTURE HOLD FOR BELTWAY?

It is unclear what the future may hold for Beltway. At this moment, the city of Chicago's rising fortunes have buoyed neighborhoods such as Beltway. Property values throughout the city soar, and a brick bungalow or split ranch that was just over $100,000 in the mid-1990s might go for $180,000 in the housing market of 2002. When I asked one Beltwayite about what the housing boom means for a young, working-class couple hoping to purchase a home in the neighborhood, she laughed: "You just have to save more money." In other words, the prospective working-class homeowner now may have to spend an extra year living with parents in a converted basement room or take an extra job or work overtime to scrape together the $20,000 you need for a 10 percent down payment. While a rise in property values means grumbling about higher property taxes, it also provides Beltway's inhabitants with a bulwark against the possibility of neighborhood turnover. It is unlikely that low-income Chicagoans looking to escape neighborhoods that are going down can afford the price tag on a Beltway bungalow these days. Beltwayites who own homes may be in no rush to dump a house that has doubled in value. The mayor's popular and highly successful plan to encourage bungalow owners to preserve and maintain older bungalow housing of the 1920s and 1930s—the Bungalow Initiative—may help Bungalow Belt homeowners take advantage of the city's housing boom and revitalize neighborhoods with aging housing stock. In time, Chicago's status as one of the most attractive cities for "young professionals" (that is, yuppies)—as rated by a recent national magazine survey—may even attract gentrifiers to the Southwest Side now that the bungalow's aesthetic merits are now more widely appreciated.

But while Chicago as a whole has benefited from the economy of recent years, the city of Chicago has witnessed other booms come and go. In the end, what goes up must come down; the only uncertainties are how quickly and for how long. In the case of Beltway, it is unlikely that younger whites will replace all of the neighborhood's aging white homeowners. Indeed, the demographics of Chicago tell us that racial change is inevitable for Beltway; the process has been well underway for two decades. Other questions remain: How quickly will the racial change affect the neighborhood's socioeconomic composition? Can Beltway maintain and reproduce social institutions over time with the changing of the racial guard? Will *working- and lower-middle-class* Hispanics and African Americans replace the working- and lower-middle-class whites who move on? Can these groups not merely coexist, but flourish as they create a racially diverse community?

I believe there can be optimism about racial integration in Beltway that comes with class stability. If property values remain strong and the new arrivals share the current population's values "about home and neighborhood," it is possible that the last garden can continue to thrive as a racially diverse working- and lower-middle-class community. Such optimism is not merely speculation, for as of today Beltway is now over 20 percent Hispanic with almost 150 African Americans residing in the neighborhood. Yet, the next challenge facing old-timers and newcomers alike will be to share community leadership and identify problems and strategies for action that resonate with all residents. Whites will need to eradicate the racist subtexts and racial explanations they rely on to explain crime, declining institutions, and the other social problems that face the neighborhood. Beltway's establishment and "the new arrivals" will have to find common ground on the basis of their shared interests as homeowners, parents, law-abiding and taxpaying citizens, firefighters and police officers, members of the working and lower-middle classes, and even Americans. Indeed the working-class blacks and whites' common social status might just be able to break down old racial barriers as class increasingly overtakes race as a salient category for working-class whites. The process may be well under way in a city where the *Defender,* Chicago's leading black paper, endorsed Richard M. Daley (that is, Mayor Richard "The Boss" Daley's son) for mayor over black candidates (in two elections) and affirmative action policies have integrated municipal jobs. If political and social expediencies, government initiatives, and the passage of time can transform even the bitterest of enemies into political bedfellows, anything is possible. Even as the racial divide shrinks ever so slowly, the class divide remains a huge, gaping chasm. After all, in the racial stereotypes Beltwayites (and indeed most Americans) rely on to make sense of the world, blacks are to be feared because they bring disorder and decay. Among white racists, of all socioeconomic backgrounds, the category of *black* is equivalent to the category *poor.* And few whites, indeed few blacks, want to live in close proximity to high poverty areas because of the serious challenges citizens and scholars know to face such communities.[2] To ignore that these "discriminatory" ideas are based on a commonsense understanding of the world, must, on some level, mitigate how we view such "racism." The great challenge that currently faces Beltway, and neighborhoods in cities across the nation, is how to fight the inequality that scars our urban landscapes.

Even the most positive view of a racially integrated Beltway leaves little opportunity for increasing tolerance of lower-income people, regardless of their race, because socioeconomic homogeneity will be needed to guide the process of racial succession. In Beltway, fostering tolerance of socioeconomic diversity remains a much more difficult challenge than creating tolerance of racial diversity. To many Beltwayites, the problem with racial diversity is really, at its core, a fear and anxiety about sharing their community with *poor* blacks, not blacks per se.

WHAT CAN WE LEARN FROM BELTWAY?

In the story of Beltway, there is a lesson about the fragility of working-class America and how uncertainty about the future feeds ugly racist and class-based antagonisms. The evolving context of race relations also reminds us how much has changed in the places where fears about racial succession drew people into the streets and led to violence and the most dangerous racial rhetoric. Over three decades after Chicago teetered on the edge of disaster, whites share their schools, workplaces, and even their neighborhoods with racial and ethnic minorities in ways that would have seemed unimaginable in 1966. There is still much to do, but few of us ever acknowledge just how far urban, working-class whites progressed on the issue of race in the late twentieth century. In 1966, a white, Polish-American city worker was not likely to have invited his African American coworker to share food in his home. Thirty-five years ago a white working-class woman would not have explained her decision to send her daughter to a racially diverse magnet high school because "it's important for her to learn how to get along with all types of people." Thirty-five years ago a white grandmother might have hidden the fact that her grandchildren are half-Mexican. Thirty-five years ago, the president of the Beltway Civic League would not have responded to the reality of black neighbors with the suggestion "You say 'hi' to them because some of them are better than the whites we've got around here." If we pay attention and look at and listen to life in Beltway, it becomes impossible to deny that progress has been made. Working-class whites now live as the racial minorities in the majority of American cities.

Today the "top cop" in the city of Chicago is African American. His predecessor was Hispanic. Of course, things have changed in Chicago, and without question, the people of Chicago's Bungalow Belt have not been untouched by these changes.

Communities such as Beltway offer a unique opportunity to learn from the mistakes of the past, and remind us how class and inequality are at the center of many of the complex problems we often subsume under the category of race. In my utopian vision of the city of the future, maybe the places where the most bloody battles over segregation were fought should be the places we go as we start the process of racial healing, as we point out just how much people have in common. I do not mean to propose that working-class blacks, whites, and Hispanics should unite against those on the bottom and those on the top. Instead, what I propose is a new way of thinking that allows individuals, community leaders, and policymakers to think beyond old categories of "neighborhood" and "race" as they build coalitions around the shared interests of homeowners, parents, city workers, young people, or taxpayers. In this account of life in Beltway, we learn how place inspires people to civic engagement around their identity as homemakers, homeowners, and taxpayers. Maybe it would be possible to spark civic engagement in other communities by inspiring individuals to align themselves with the broader status interests of homeowners, parents, young people, and taxpayers?

As I write this book, I have carefully tried to negotiate the roles of scholar, intellectual, and advocate. In the end, even though many readers may label me an apologist for the white working class, I must declare that the greatest lesson I have learned from the last garden is that the much maligned white working-class neighborhood possesses elements that are precious and worth defending. My hope is that the best features of life in the last garden can be shared with other communities.

For in spite of such neighborhoods' complicated histories and failures, these are the places where a tattered yet cherished notion of an idealized America and community coexists with people's everyday lives. Even the "objective" scholarly observer cannot help but be moved by that idealism, and at the end of the day, such idealism is precious because from it can grow the idyllic possibilities that America promises. If the people of the last garden can believe in America, why cannot the rest of us? The challenge then becomes how we can reconfigure, retool, and reimagine our cities for the America of the twenty-first century.

IN THE FIELD

My parents are not native-born Americans. My father attended school in New York City after moving to the United States from the island of Chios in Greece. My mother attended high school and college in Boston, but she was born and raised on the island nation of St. Lucia. Given my parents' exotic lineage, on paper at least I am the daughter of immigrants. But my parents' lives raising my sisters and brother and me in America bears little resemblance to the archetypal "immigrant" story. Both my parents are from affluent families in their homelands, and they both came to the United States to study. My father eventually earned a Master's degree in Engineering from CUNY (the poor man's Yale), and my mother holds a Master's Degree in Education from Lesley College. Most of my childhood was spent in Lexington, Massachusetts, an affluent suburb of Boston that is home to Harvard professors. During my childhood, summers were filled with soccer games, trips to the Cape, and private swimming lessons.

To be sure, my family raised me to take great pride in my ethnic heritage (I am Greek Orthodox), and I have traveled to my parents' respective homelands, but most of my own life has been spent sheltered in the comfortable world of the suburbs and the "ivory towers" of elite universities. That said, I also understood that my Greek surname, olive complexion, and black, curly hair marked me as "ethnic" and thus something of an outsider in spite of my social and economic privilege.

Even though I had cousins who lived in the famous Greek enclaves of Astoria in Queens, New York, and Lowell, Massachusetts, my own ties to such places were tenuous at best. But such a diverse heritage has helped me be more self-conscious about how I view the world, and my in-between ethnic status helps me notice things "natives" might be more likely to miss. (My father taught me my first lesson about negotiating between different worlds. He is one of those rare individuals who can talk to anyone and truly counts people from a wide variety of backgrounds among his friends. He is equally comfortable in settings where he is surrounded by white collars or blue ones.) No doubt, my fractured status as the daughter of immigrants facilitated my entry into Beltway, a world populated by people who themselves were just a generation or two away from ancestors who had come to America from some place else. In "the last garden," I found I could speak easily with people about their rather self-conscious identity as Americans. Class proved a less difficult barrier to overcome than I first expected because anyone who looks like me, can make spinach pie, and can tell stories about working in her family's restaurant *must* be a full-fledged member of the white ethnic world. As a result, Beltwayites often assumed that my socioeconomic background was closer to their own than it truly was. Also, in the neighborhood, I often found myself playing a role familiar from my upbringing: that of the respectful and helpful young woman. On my visits to the neighborhood, I made my way to the kitchen where I would offer to help with the food or the dishes. Indeed, I always tried to avoid going to people's homes empty-handed. The fact that my husband and I enjoy cooking and eating was probably our most useful "skill" for fieldwork.

In Beltway, I never talked about my education and rarely mentioned my aspiration to become a university professor. One of my close friends from Beltway, who did know about my studies, complimented me one day for downplaying my connections to the academic world. She said,

"I like how you never make me feel bad or stupid [because of your education]." I never shared my views on politics or social policy, not as a result of conscious concealment, but simply because no one ever asked me for my opinion. Most Beltwayites were quite flattered by my genuine interest in their views, and so there was little time for asking me about how I felt about matters. I do not believe residents ever saw me as a total insider, but they did come to trust me as someone who would do her best to tell their story. As a fieldworker, I took on the charge of documenting local culture and explaining how Beltwayites make sense of their world. I suspect that people from the neighborhood assumed I agreed with them on matters when I often did not. However, as a researcher, I have no interest in arguing with the people whose lives I am trying to chronicle. In my role as participant observer, I always try to foster a sense of empathy, not sympathy, for people whose circumstances are familiar yet quite distinct from my own.

NOTES

INTRODUCTION

1. The works of the Chicago School and scholars such as Whyte (1943), Gans (1962), Suttles (1968), Halle (1984), and Rieder (1985) guided me most during those first days in Beltway. Indeed, to the credit of my predecessors, I recognized and rediscovered much of what they had already documented in previous studies of the white working class. Scholars from the University of Chicago pioneered the use of anthropological research methods in urban settings in the United States during the early part of the twentieth century. This influential intellectual movement is known as the Chicago School.

2. Because economic changes caused by deindustrialization and the decline of manufacturing have shifted more workers into the service sector, so-called working-class Americans are now less likely to work in factories or on shop floors. As a result, terms such as blue-collar and working-class have become more ambiguous given that workers in the low end of the service sector have collars that are likely to be colored white and pink. And yet when we look at workers' earnings and benefits, we see that low-end white-collar jobs have more in common with the old blue-collar jobs (and indeed may be worse given the absence of unions and mandated benefits) than with professional-class white-collar jobs held by college-educated workers. As Michèle Lamont notes (and I also observed) these blurring distinctions between the service/technology sector and traditional working-class jobs have led to the popularity of the term

"lower-middle-class" among the people whose income and education classify them as working-class. In the 1990 U.S. Census, 40 percent of the currently employed population over 25 years of age were high school graduates employed in a blue-collar or lower-white-collar-occupations.

3. Lamont (2000): 2.

4. During the 1960s and 1970s a more racialized picture of the inner city dominated urban sociology. Inspired (or enraged) by the work of Oscar Lewis (1951, 1965, 1966) and the Moynihan Report debate, a legion of ethnographers descended on America's black ghettoes in search of the culture of poverty. See Liebow (1967), Hannerz (1969), Stack (1974), and Anderson (1978). Wilson's (1978, 1987) now classic formulation of the underclass and Massey and Denton's (1992) impressive analysis of racial segregation further solidified scholarly interest in the experiences of poor minorities in urban settings.

5. In 2000, of the 31,139,000 Americans living in poverty, 14,572,000 (47 percent) were non-hispanic whites.

6. "The transfiguration of the ancient peasant land hunger occurred in the context of the immigrants' quest for security, respectability, community, and status in a society that questioned both their ability and their worth. The purchase of a new home, the Lithuanian newspaper *Lietuva* subsequently editorialized in 1913, was not only 'one of the best ways to get ahead,' it was also a way of honoring your nationality; it was a patriotic as well as a profitable practice." (Hirsch 1983: 171). Historians such as Hirsch (1983), Sugrue (1996), and McGreevey (1996) and sociologists such as Rieder (1985) and Gans (1962) have written about working-class urban whites' "peasant" sensibilities.

7. Beltway is a pseudonym. The names of people, street names, places, schools, and other identifying characteristics have been changed to protect the identities of those who participated in this study. The names of city officials such as Mayor Daley, Chicago Public School CEO Paul Vallas, and Congressman William Lipinski have not been changed. The aldermen's names have been changed. I have tried to match the ethnicity of the pseudonyms with the true names of informants. Also, even though Beltway is a fabricated name, the true "Beltway's" name is connected to the railroad industry that has played such an important role in the area's development.

8. See Suttles (1972).

9. Based on comments from Michèle Lamont, November 1999.

10. Grossman (2001): 1A.

11. Hirsch (1983), 171.

12. Morenoff and Sampson (1997) document the links between race, crime, poverty, and the spread of Chicago's ghetto.

13. The residents who stayed (out of choice or not) represent a highly self-selected segment of the population and one should not be surprised by fairly consistent responses as to how residents feel about the community and why they want to stay. It is also important to point out that the policy requiring municipal workers to reside within the city limits has made the stability possible.

14. See Cronon (1991) for a discussion of how the "windy city" referred to the overenthusiastic praise of Chicago's boosters. The nickname was actually bestowed by *New York Sun* editor Charles Dana in 1893. He was tired of hearing long-winded politicians boasting about the World Columbian Exhibition, held in Chicago that year.

15. Berger (1967): 21.

16. Logan and Molotch (1987): 100.

17. Parish life has been a necessary omission in this study. The priests in the neighborhood were unwilling to grant interviews, and the times and limitations of research made it difficult to collect data. In a sense, parish life was quite central to people's lives as Catholics, but the active role of the priest within the larger community depended heavily on each priest's particular skills and inclinations. The most active church leader in the neighborhood (on civic issues) at the time of the study was the minister of the local Methodist church. In years past, this had not been the case; various Catholic clergy had taken a strong role in community life. Over the years activist priests had even tried to encourage local residents to hold more progressive attitudes on the issue of race.

18. Community studies have long been dominated by the lone wolf male ethnographer who gained entry into the field by socializing in bars and walking the streets. As a result, gaining entry into the worlds controlled and maintained by women has proven difficult, if not impossible. It is not surprising that in the classic community studies the voices of women have fallen into the background or, in many cases, been silent. Consider works such as Whyte's account of the North End, Liebow and Hannerz's Washington D,C., Suttles's Taylor Street, Rieder's Canarsie, Anderson's Village-Northton, and Duneier's Hyde Park. However, women as caretakers of the domestic realm are important guardians of local culture. No doubt the neglect of women in urban ethnographies goes some way to explaining the undertheorizing of local culture in much

of the community studies' scholarship. Notably, Young and Wilmott's (1957) study of families in England is an important exception. Young and Wilmott offer an evocative account of family life, particularly from the perspectives of young mothers and their "mums."

19. I explore how low-income whites construct motherhood, meaning, and respectability in my current research with Kathryn Edin set in Philadelphia.

CHAPTER ONE. RETHINKING RACE IN THE ETHNIC WHITE ENCLAVE

1. "Bungalows, historians tell us, were a cornerstone of the democraticization of the American residence that accompanied the Progressive Era at the end of the nineteenth century. They represented an attempt to reconcile the inclusion of new technologies like indoor plumbing and electricity, which added considerable cost to a house, with affordability by downsizing the typical family home" (Conklin 2001: C5). For a fascinating historical and architectural account of the significance of the Chicago bungalow, see Bigott (2001).

2. *A Little Known Story of a Land Called Clearing* (Chicago: Robert Milton Hill: 1982): 158.

3. Ibid.

4. Ibid.

5. "In Chicago a majority of the bungalows were built between 1915 and 1930. Mass construction, when entire blocks became bungalowized, occurred in 1926–27. The boom, killed by the Depression, also ushered in new sales techniques such as telephone solicitation and the use of model houses. The next surge in home building came after World War II, and it gave us the raised ranch, a style of house that is similar to the bungalow. However, the central theme of the raised ranch is less is more, and though it included more modern conveniences such as central air, there were fewer windows, no wide overhangs, and not as many ornate features such as stained-glass windows and custom masonry. Bungalows assumed a variety of designs in the United States" (Conklin 2001: C5).

6. While the ethnic composition of Beltway remained roughly the same, another group of migrants entered the mix after the war. According to Robert Platt who compiled a report on the Hastings Public School in 1946, the ancestry of most students was "German and Polish but most students who came after the war were mainly from Adair County in the hills of Kentucky with a sprin-

kling of others from Indiana and Tennessee." The parents of the children at Hastings were mostly factory workers, according to Platt. The migrants from the southern states settled in the Village area where many of their descendants reside today.

7. Ehrenhalt (1995): 92.

8. Ibid.

9. Ibid.

10. In contrast to the Marxist view of the traditional worker, the so-called blue-collar aristocrats now seek satisfaction outside the workplace while deserting the political realm and accepting the inherent meaninglessness of their work. Consumption is becoming a privileged sphere in which one finds self-satisfaction. "An update and critique of Goldethorpe and Lockwood's work (1969) is offered by Devine (1992), who suggests that the British working class is less privatized than they had suggested. As documented by previous research, blue-collar workers put family above work and find greater satisfaction in family than do upper-middle-class men. Family is the realm of life that gives the intrinsic satisfaction and validation that are crucial when work is not rewarding" (Lamont 2000: 30). See Halle (1984), Logan and Molotch (1987), Perin (1977, 1988), Gottdiener (1985), and Hummon (1990) for an analysis of homeownership and class .

11. Hirsch (1983) provides a historical account of a similar incident in Chicago's Trumbull Park. Hirsch writes, "Some events, such as the black attempt to use the park's swimming pool, came to be seen as acts of sexual aggression. Given working-class whites' understanding of community (intimate contact was a necessary corollary to entry into the neighborhood), the one naturally flowed from the other." Sharing the pool seemed like a sort of sexual assault that threatened to erode working-class ethnics' claims to whiteness through the possibility of interracial marriage and "miscegenation." Their fear of losing their identity as whites was clearly revealed by their overwhelming concern with the prospect of interracial marriage or sexual assault in transition areas.

12. Hirsch (1983): 197

13. Ibid., 194–95.

14. "The merging of the ethnics who shared a common American past and neighborhood demonstrates the malleability of ethnicity in the absence of striking color differences. Historians have also noted the ardent ambition to own a lot of land on the part of the Irish, Italian, and Slavic immigrants" (Hirsch 1983: 195).

15. Hirsch (1983): 197–98.

16. There is a small Protestant population in the neighborhood, and many local Protestants can trace their families back to the area's first white settlers. The vast majority of Beltway residents are Catholic.

17. Census figures for 1990 indicate that 7.5 percent of the Beltway population describe themselves as Hispanic. The first wave of Mexican American arrivals (just over 90 percent of Beltway's Hispanic population) report that they speak English "well" or "very well." Indeed, Latinos have slightly higher levels of education than their white neighbors.

18. The idea that Mexicans are more like an ethnic group than a racial one is unique to the context of race and ethnic relations in Chicago. Mexicans are seen as "transnational migrants" in New York while they are seen as a race in California. Mexicans' being viewed in Chicago as yet another piece of the city's ethnic mosaic has eased their transition and makes them even more preferable to African Americans. At the same time, they are not completely protected from the destructive role of racism, and whites' willingness to share their neighborhoods with Mexicans offers some hope for the nature of race relations. Based on comments from Philip Kasinitz, July 2001.

19. Rieder (1985): 85.

20. See Kornblum (1974) for an informative discussion of relations between Poles and Mexicans in the steel industry in South Chicago. The racial identity of Mexicans is a central question in this debate. There are some who view these most recent immigrants as the Jews, Italians, and Greeks of this historical moment. Concern is growing that the racial order of American society may become of system of whites and "browns" against blacks.

21. See Massey and Denton (1992) for a comparison between the racial segregation faced by Hispanics and the level faced by blacks.

22. The shift into white-collar work—clean brain work—continues to improve job quality all the time, but earnings for most occupations have not improved in recent years; indeed, earnings in occupations with low skill requirements have declined. "In 1996, a typical white male in his fifties with a bachelor's degree had earnings of about $51,000, and he was almost certain to have health insurance. In the previous 10 years, however, his earnings had grown by only 7 percent, and if he read the newspaper, he knew there was a possibility that he soon would be let go. A white-male high school graduate of similar age had no doubts on this point. He was making $31,300, about $2000 to $3000 less (in 1997

dollars) than he had made when he was forty, and there was almost a 10 percent chance that he did not have health insurance. As far as he could tell, his children would have to go to college to have a chance at the middle class" (Levy, 1998: 92).

23. Gans, 1991.

24. In 1999 the median family income in the United States was $48,950. At the time of publication, the U.S. Census 2000 numbers for Beltway were not available, but given historical trends, one would expect median household income in Beltway to hover just below the national median family income for 2000.

25. See Lasch (1991), chap. 11, for a more detailed discussion. In 1969, John Goldethorpe, David Lockwood, and their colleagues published what was to become a classic study of the British working class, *The Affluent Worker in the Class Structure.* They offered a critique of the "proletarian embourgeoisment" thesis and proposed that British postwar workers are less allied with the bourgeoisie in their class interests (as traditional Marxists had argued) than engaged in instrumental behavior: they are selling their work to the highest bidder while turning all their emotional commitments toward family life.

26. Uchitelle (2000).

27. "It might seem natural to assume that if wages and family incomes grew slowly after 1973, living standards grew slowly as well. Surprisingly, this assumption is wrong, at least by standard measures. Between 1973 and 1989, real consumer expenditure per capita grew at a rate of 34 percent per decade. Much of the new money went to such necessities as housing, medical care, and utilities. Still, the growth in spending per capita was faster than in the Eisenhower 1950s. The contradiction is easily reconciled. The post-1973 growth in consumption per capita did not reflect a booming economy in the 1950s sense, but rather two national trends: the growing proportion of the population (specifically of middle-aged women) that worked and our increased willingness to take on debt." See Levy (1997): 50–51.

28. As quoted in Wolfe (1998): 10.

29. Ibid., p. 2.

30. Based on comments from Gerald Suttles, December 1993.

31. See Hartigan (1999) for a discussion of how white Detroiters use and live race in their neighborhoods. In addition, see Lamont (2000) for her fascinating discussion of "euphemized racism."

32. By all accounts, local law enforcement were aware of the fact that members of gangs such as the Popes, Two-Sixers, and Satan's Disciples were involved in low-level drug dealing, had access to guns, and regularly attacked or "jumped" other teenagers. Garage break-ins were the most common crime to involve gang members and adult residents.

33. These findings are quite consistent with the work of Mercer Sullivan in his comparative ethnographic study of at-risk youth and delinquents in three New York City neighborhoods (1989).

34. Alinsky (1969): ix–x.

CHAPTER TWO.
A PRECIOUS CORNER OF THE WORLD

1. See Jackson (1994) for his discussion of the sense of place.

2. See Tuan (1980), (1977), and (1974) for his discussion of landscape and the sense of place and the conceptualization of home.

3. Logan and Molotch (1987): 19.

4. Sampson, Raudenbush, and Earls (1997).

5. Cox (1981): 433.

6. Janowitz and Suttles (1977): 260.

7. Zukin (1993): 16.

8. In the end, Robert Park and Ernest Burgess's Darwinist-inspired studies and Louis Wirth's grave prognostications about community lost fail to explain a persistent empirical phenomenon: people's attachment to community (Cohen 1985). Studies of working-class urban neighborhoods [Whyte (1943), Gans (1962), Suttles (1968), Kornblum (1974), Young and Wilmott (1957)], and of rural communities [Coles (1967), Erickson (1976), Peshkin (1978), Cochrane (1987), Bell (1994)] all show that communities can and do become continuing loci of sentimental identification. Even in suburban Levittown, whose residents are far from folk-like, Gans (1982) found at least the potential for identification with community that might have arisen should something have threatened the community as a whole.

9. For a more detailed discussion of this work see Patillo-McCoy, *Black Picket Fences* (1999), her ethnographic account of the lower-middle-class black Chicago neighborhood of Groveland. This research was completed as part of

the Comparative Neighborhood Study Project through which my own study of Beltway was conducted.

10. Rieder (1985): 84.

11. Putnam (1995): 65.

12. Grossman and Leroux (1996).

13. "There are some that attempt to document the role of local culture in the symbolic construction of community identity [see Firey (1945), Strauss (1961), Lofland (1973), Tuan (1974), Krase (1976), Karp, Stone, and Yoels (1977), Suttles (1984), and Hummon (1990)]. Local culture is not a simple reflection of community circumstances; instead local culture reflects shared beliefs and values that shape popular orientations and social processes" (Hummon, 1990: 45). For a discussion of popular belief and sentiment toward community see Gelfant (1954), Hadden and Barton (1979), Marx (1984), Sussman (1985), and Hummon (1990).

14. Rieder (1985): 61.

15. Hedbige (1979): 3. For other scholarly treatments of hip-hop, graffiti, and street culture see Tricia Rose's (1994) *Black Noise* and Susan Phillips's (1999) *Wallbangin'*. Hedbige's work provides an excellent and more general theoretical overview of youth subcultures as revolutionary endeavors in the intellectual tradition of the Birmingham School.

16. A more detailed analysis of the murders can be found in Patrick Carr's dissertation, "Keeping Up Appearances," Department of Sociology, University of Chicago, June 1998.

17. This ethnographic account of the murders was originally presented as a paper I coauthored with Patrick Carr, titled "Denial and Accountability: The Case of the Powell-Harvey Murders," at the 1996 meeting of the American Society of Criminology.

18. A more detailed discussion of informal social control in Beltway can be found in Patrick Carr's unpublished paper "The New Parochialism: The Implications of the Beltway Case for Arguments concerning Informal Social Control."

CHAPTER THREE. HOME, SWEET HOME

1. Conklin (2001): C5.

2. "In Chicago most bungalows were built between 1915–1940. Mass construction when entire blocks were bungalowized occurred in 1926–1927. The boom, killed by the Depression, heralded the use of the model home and phone

solicitation as sales techniques. Another surge in home construction came after World War II and brought the 'raised ranch,' a style of house very similar to the bungalow. However, the central theme of the raised ranch was 'less is more,' and though it included modern conveniences such as central air, there were fewer windows, no wide overhangs, and not as many ornate features such as custom masonry" (Conklin 2001: C5). Most houses in Beltway are technically raised ranches, but Beltway is still part of the city's Bungalow Belt, and I will use the term to evoke the working-class imagery of this architectural style.

3. Ehrenhalt (1995): 90. Even though Ehrenhalt's analysis recalls a mythic past of Chicago's Bungalow Belt, his account of a lost way of life in Chicago's neighborhoods provides an interesting reference point for this study of life in modern-day Beltway.

4. A 1978 study by Coleman and Rainwater investigated the meaning of class for a sample of Americans in a variety of occupations and found that for most people income level and standard of living (the houses they lived in, the cars they drove, the recreations and vacations they could afford) were the dominant considerations in where they placed themselves in the socioeconomic ladder. Thus status image is based on items that constitute life outside of work. In Bourdieu's formulation of cultural capital, high culture is a device by which the dominant class excludes the dominated classes in capitalism. In *Distinction* (1984), Bourdieu's target is the problematic use of notions of taste as a sort of naturally occurring phenomenon to mark and maintain social boundaries, whether these lines are being drawn by the dominant or dominated classes. Bourdieu goes on to present a three-zone model of cultural tastes: "legitimate" taste, "middle brow" taste, and "popular taste." Within Bourdieu's ethnographic study of taste in French society, the working-class aesthetic is a dominated aesthetic constantly obliged to define itself by reference to the dominant aesthetic. In fact, according to Bourdieu, the working class is so dominated and subordinate that its members are less able than the upper or middle classes to adopt a specifically aesthetic view upon objects whose constitution and definition involve an aesthetic judgment. Economic constraints and the disposition of working-class habitus produce an adaptive response which is distinguished by the relative absence of aesthetic choice-making: Bourdieu writes, "Nothing is more alien to working-class women than the typically bourgeois idea of making each object in the home the occasion for an aesthetic choice" (1984: 45). Further, he is emphatic that "income

produces choices—or their refusal—only in conjunction with a habitus that is already in harmony with the economic limitations in which it functions." Bourdieu (1984) contends that consumption-related endeavors—i.e., aesthetic taste—are so central to everyday life that a hierarchy of tastes is among the most important mechanisms for social reproduction and class subordination.

Randall Collins describes working-class culture as a dilution of elites' inward-oriented, cultivated aesthetic, and moral values. To Collins, a working-class culture in general emphasizes group conformity, localism, and a reified attitude to cultural objects and is a static response to dominant class culture . Paul Willis (1977) offers an explanation of working-class culture that leaves some possibility for creative resistance, but even this celebration of the values of the virility (to use Bourdieu's term) falters in that it leads to social reproduction in the end.

5. Halle (1984): 100. Halle grapples with blue-collar workers' variable and contradictory notions of class identity, status-group membership, and home-ownership. He argues that the "Imperium" workers ("Imperium" is the pseudonym for the factory he studied) hold two images of class. Their first image, what Halle terms the "ideal of the working man," emerges out of a politics centering on work and the union. Their second image of class centers on life outside of work and takes a variety of forms. However, homeownership sharpens people's interests, for many issues are seen as affecting the values of their houses and the levels of property taxes they pay (225).

6. Jackson (1985): 51. Jackson's work offers an important historical account of the rise of the suburbs.

7. Halle (1984): 11.

8. In 1990, Beltway's median house value was $101,709; in 1999, $124,000; in 2000, $119,000; and in 2001, $141,000.

9. The anthropologist Constance Perin has written extensively about the significance of home-ownership in contemporary American life. See Perin (1977). The significance of home-ownership is further reinforced by government policies that offer tax breaks and mortgage programs to encourage citizens' investment in property.

10. See Taub et al. (1984) for a more detailed discussion of how class influences the ways in which urban dwellers feel about neighborhood change.

11. Riesman (1958): 390, quoted in Perin (1988): 31.

12. Cooper (1974). Steedman's (1994) impressive autobiography/biography of her working-class childhood/mother in 1950s London, titled *Landscape for a Good Woman,* provides a breathtaking account of gender, respectability, class, and motherhood. Steedman's story also provides anecdotal evidence for the power of gendered notions of class-structured ideals of respectability.

13. Oakley (1974): 44. Gullestad (1984) notes that among middle-class cultures cleanliness is taken for granted; one presumes people and places to be clean until the opposite is evident. In this way, cleanliness is important in both milieus. The difference is that in middle-class cultures the distinction is applied when the standard is too low. In working-class culture, it is explicitly and often applied when the speaker finds the state of affairs to be too high or just right, as well as when it is too low. Part of the reason for this difference may be that standards of cleanliness are more threatened in lower-class settings because of the dirty nature of work and the lower standard of housing. Steedman discusses the significance of cleanliness in respectability as well.

14. Steedman (1994): 34. The intimate connections of gender, identity, and dwelling are best epitomized in the well-known dictum: "A woman's place is in the home." The social and cultural construction of the home as a peculiarly woman's place is relatively recent. The rapid separation of public life and paid employment from the home, followed by the segregation of suburban middle-class life from the city, led to the home being transformed into a place primarily devoted to privacy, domesticity, procreation, and consumption [Hadden and Barton (1979), Wright (1980), Loyd (1982), Hayden (1984), Wetering (1984), Jackson (1985), and Fishman (1987)]. Ideal roles for women as caretakers of the home increasingly focused on family nurturance, housework, and the expressive symbolization of middle-class life and status through domestic consumption (Loyd 1982).

15. Steedman (1994): 43. For fascinating discussions of the significance of domesticity and homemaking, see Gullestad (1984) and Oakley (1974). Also see Collins (1990) for a discussion of how women of different classes use housework to display status . Collins contends that working-class women "are more obsessed with the cleanliness of their home for they are most likely to identify status with housework and the appearance of the house itself (218–19)." He explains that while middle-class women came to see employment as the standard for feminist liberation, working-class women viewed work as an economic necessity. For working-class women then, the middle-class ideal to which they aspire is not feminism but to be a full-time homemaker whose affluence has liberated her from the paid labor force.

CHAPTER FOUR.
FOR COUNTRY AND HOME

1. Rieder (1985): 36.

2. Ibid.

3. Proposition 187 was passed in 1994 and was put on "hold" by a federal court, but the vote helped set the stage for a national debate on immigration legislation in Congress.

4. Police claim that a new gang has started operating in the neighborhood under the name PWA (Polacks with attitude). The gang, made up of new Poles, allegedly specializes in stealing car radios. .

5. According to the U.S. Census, over the past 40 years the majority of Beltway residents were Polish, Lithuanian, German, Irish, and Italian.

6. Voters tossed Bilandic out of the mayor's office in favor of Byrne two decades ago when the former failed to clear heavy snows vigorously enough and the latter made political hay of it.

7. While Beltwayites start public gatherings and meetings with the Pledge of Allegiance, in Mary Patillo-McCoy's (1999) account of life in Groveland (a lower-middle-class African American community), meetings start with prayers. For a more detailed discussion of the significance of the sacred in public events see *Black Picket Fences.*

8. Gans (1991): 16.

9. Such civic/religious events provide an important function for the white ethnics and their self-conscious claims to being American. In these events, the once contradictory notions of American and ethnic white Catholic become reconciled.

10. Bourdieu (1984).

11. Anderson (1983): 135.

12. Ibid.

13. Ibid., 121, 143.

14. Ibid., 145.

CONCLUSION

1. Based on correspondence with Herbert Gans, February 2001.

2. Although, as Michèle Lamont (2000) notes, working-class African Americans express much more sympathy for those "below" than working-class whites do. See her discussion of the "disciplined self" versus the "caring self."

BIBLIOGRAPHY

Alinsky, Saul D. 1969 [1946]. *Reveille for Radicals.* New York: Vintage Books.
———. 1971. *Rules for Radicals.* New York: Random House.
Allen, J., and Doreen Massey. 1995. *Geographical Worlds.* Oxford: Oxford University Press.
Anderson, Benedict. 1983. *Imagined Communities.* New York: Verso.
Anderson, Elijah. 1978. *A Place on the Corner.* Chicago: University of Chicago Press.
———. 1990. *Streetwise.* Chicago: University of Chicago Press.
Anderson, Nels. 1923. *The Hobo.* Chicago: University of Chicago Press.
Andre, Rae. 1981. *Homemakers: The Forgotten Workers.* Chicago: University of Chicago Press.
Arendt, Hannah. 1958. *The Human Condition.* Chicago: University of Chicago Press.
Aronowitz, Stanley. 1973. *False Promises: The Shaping of American Working-Class Consciousness.* New York: McGraw-Hill.
Bachelard, Gaston. 1969. *The Poetics of Space.* Boston: Beacon Press.
Becker, Howard. 1963. *The Outsiders.* New York: Free Press.
Bell, C., and D. Newby. 1976. "Communion, Communalism, Class, and Community Action: The Sources of New Urban Politics." In *Social Areas in Cities,* edited by D. Herbert and R. Johnson. Chichester: Wiley.
Bell, Michael Mayerfeld. 1994. *Childerley.* Chicago: University of Chicago Press.

Bender, Thomas. 1975. *Toward an Urban Vision.* Lexington: University of Kentucky Press.

Berger, Bennett. 1960. *Working Class Suburb.* Berkeley and Los Angeles: University of California Press.

Berger, Peter. 1967. *The Sacred Canopy.* New York: Anchor Books. Doubleday.

Berger, Peter, and Thomas Luckmann. 1966. *The Social Construction of Reality.* New York: Anchor Books. Doubleday.

Berk, Sarah Fenstermaker. 1980. *Women and Household Labor.* Beverly Hills, Calif.: Sage.

———. 1985. *The Gender Factor: The Apportionment of Work in American Households.* New York: Plenum.

Biddis, R. A. 1991. *A Sense of Place.* Oxford: Oxford University Press.

Bigott, Joseph. 2001. *From Cottage to Bungalow: Housing and the Working Classes in Metropolitan Chicago from 1869 to 1929.* Chicago: University of Chicago Press.

Bourdieu, Pierre. 1977. *Outline of the Theory of Practice.* Cambridge: Cambridge University Press.

———. 1984. *Distinction: A Social Critique of the Evaluation of Taste.* Cambridge: Harvard University Press.

Buttimer, Anne. 1980. "Home, Reach, and the Sense of Place." In *The Human Experience of Space and Place,* edited by Anne Buttimer and David Seamon. New York: St. Martin's Press.

Calhoun, Craig. 1983. "The Radicalism of Tradition: Community Strength or Venerable Disguise and Borrowed Language?" *American Journal of Sociology* 88: 86–94.

Carr, Patrick. 2002. "The New Parochialism: The Implications of the Beltway Case for Arguments Concerning Social Control." Unpublished paper.

Casey, Edward. 1993. *Getting Back into Place.* Bloomington: Indiana University Press.

Castells, Manuel. 1976. "Theory and Ideology in Urban Sociology." In *Urban Sociology: Critical Essays,* edited by C. G. Pickvance. New York: St. Martin's Press.

———. 1979. *The Urban Question.* Cambridge: MIT Press.

———. 1983. *The City and the Grassroots.* Berkeley and Los Angeles: University of California Press.

Chapman, Dennis. 1955. *The Home and Social Status*. New York: Routledge and Kegan Paul.

Chauncey, George. 1994. *Gay New York*. New York: Basic Books.

Chodorow, Nancy. 1978. *The Reproduction of Mothering*. Berkeley and Los Angeles: University of California Press.

Cochrane, Timothy. 1987. "Place, People, and Folklore: An Isle Royale Case Study." *Western Folklore* 46: 1–20.

Cohen, Anthony. 1985. *The Symbolic Construction of Community*. London: Routledge.

Coleman, Richard, and Lee Rainwater. 1978. *Social Standing in America*. New York: Basic Books.

Coles, Robert. 1967. *Migrants, Sharecroppers, and Mountaineers*. Boston: Little, Brown.

Collins, Randall. 1975. *Conflict Sociology*. New York: Academic.

———. 1990. "Women and the Production of Status Cultures." In *Cultivating Differences,* edited by Michèle Lamont and Marcel Fournier. Chicago: University of Chicago Press.

Conklin, Mike. 2001. "Year of the Bungalow." *Chicago Tribune,* April 6.

Cooper, Clare. 1974. "The House as a Symbol of Self." In *Designing for Human Behavior,* edited by Jon Lang et al. Stroudsburg, Pa.: Dowden, Hutchinson, and Ross.

Coser, Lewis. 1971. *Masters of Sociological Thought,* New York: Harcourt Brace Jovanovich.

Cowan, Ruth Schwartz. 1983. *More Work for Mother*. New York: Basic Books.

Cox, Harvey. 1965. *The Secular City*. New York: Macmillan.

Cox, Kevin. 1981. "Capitalism and Conflict around the Communal Living Place." In *Urbanization and Urban Planning in a Capitalist Society,* edited by Michael Dear and Allen J. Scott. New York: Methuen.

Cressy, Paul. 1932. *The Taxi-Dance Hall*. Montclair, N.J.: Patterson Smith.

Cronon, William. 1991. Nature's Metropolis. New York: W. W. Norton.

Csikzentmihalyi, Mihaly, and Eugene Rochberg-Halton. 1981. *The Meaning of Things*. Cambridge: Cambridge University Press.

Dean, John. 1951. "The Ghosts of Home-Ownership." *Journal of Social Issues* 7: 59–68.

Devine, Flora. 1992. *Affluent Workers Revisited*. Edinburgh: Edinburgh University Press.

Dingemas, J. 1975. "Urbanization of Suburbia: Renaissance of the Row House."*Landscape* 1: 19–31.

Dixon, Penelope. 1991. *Mothers and Mothering.* New York: Garland.

Douglas, Mary. 1982. *Food in the Social Order.* New York: Russell Sage.

Duncan, James. 1973. "Landscape Taste as a Symbol of Group Identity," *Geographical Review* 63: 334–55.

———, ed. 1982. *Housing and Identity.* New York: Holmes and Meier.

Duneier, Mitchell. 1992. *Slim's Table.* Chicago: University of Chicago Press.

Dunham, Jan. 1991. "Men and Women in the City: The Effects of Gender, Work, and Family on Local Community Life." Ph.D. Dissertation, University of Chicago.

Durkheim, Emile. 1969. *The Division of Labor.* New York: Free Press.

Ehrenhalt, Alan. 1995. *The Lost City.* New York: Basic Books.

Erickson, Kai. 1976. *Everything in Its Path.* New York: Simon and Schuster.

Eyles, John. 1985. *Sense of Place.* Warrington, U.K.: Silverbrook Press.

Fantasia, Rick. 1988. *Cultures of Solidarity.* Berkeley and Los Angeles: University of California Press.

Firey, Walter. 1945. "Sentiment and Symbolism as Economic Variables." *American Sociological Review* 5: 140–148.

Fischer, Claude. 1977. "Comments on the History and Study of Community." In *Networks and Places,* edited by Claude Fischer et al. New York: Free Press.

———. 1982. *To Dwell among Friends.* Chicago: University of Chicago Press.

———. 1984. *The Urban Experience.* New York: Harcout Brace Jovanovich.

Fischer, Claude, and C. Ann Stueve. 1977. *Authentic Community: The Role of Place in Modern Life.* New York: Free Press.

Fishman, Robert. 1987. *Bourgeois Utopias.* New York: Basic Books.

Fried, Mark. 1963. "Grieving for Lost Home." In *The Urban Condition,* edited by L.J. Duhl. New York: Basic Books.

Fried, Mark, and Peggy Gleicher. 1961. "Some Sources of Residential Satisfaction in an Urban Slum." *Journal of the American Institute of Planners* 27: 305–15.

Gamm, Gerald. 1999. *Urban Exodus: Why the Jews Left Boston and the Catholics Stayed.* Cambridge: Harvard University Press.

Gans, Herbert. 1962. *The Urban Villagers.* New York: Free Press.

———. 1982. *The Levittowners.* Chicago: University of Chicago Press.

———. 1990. "Preface." In *Cultivating Differences,* edited by Michele Lamont and Marcel Fournier. Chicago: University of Chicago Press.

———. 1991. *Middle American Individualism.* Oxford: Oxford University Press.

Geertz, Clifford. 1973. *The Interpretation of Cultures.* New York: Basic Books.

Gelfant, Blanche. 1954. *The American City Novel.* Norman: University of Oklahoma Press.

Gerson, Kathleen, Ann Stueve, and Claude Fischer. 1977. "Attachment to Place." In *Networks and Places,* edited by Claude Fischer et al. New York: Free Press.

Gerth, Hans, and C. Wright Mills, eds. 1946. *From Max Weber: Essays in Sociology.* New York: Oxford University Press.

Giddens, Anthony. 1973. *The Class Structure of the Advanced Societies.* New York: Harper and Row.

Gillian, Rose. 1993. *Feminism and Geography.* Cambridge, U.K.: Polity Press.

Ginsburg, Faye D. 1989. *Contested Lives.* Berkeley and Los Angeles: University of California Press.

Glaser, Barney, and Anslem Strauss. 1967. *The Discovery of Grounded Theory.* Chicago: Aldine.

Goffman, Erving. 1959. *The Presentation of Self in Everyday Life.* New York: Anchor Books.

Goldethorpe, John, David Lockwood, and Jennifer Platt. 1968. *The Affluent Worker.* Cambridge: Cambridge University Press.

Gottdiener, Mark. 1983. "Some Theoretical Issues in Growth Control." *Urban Affairs Quarterly* 17: 55–73.

———. 1985. *The Social Production of Urban Space.* Austin: University of Texas Press.

Greer, Scott. 1962. *The Emerging City.* New York: Free Press.

Griswold, Wendy. 1986. *Renaissance Revivals: City Comedy and Revenge Tragedy in London Theatre 1576–1980.* Chicago: University of Chicago Press.

Grossman, Ron. 2001. "America's Vision Has Always Had a Blind Spot." *Chicago Tribune,* June 17.

Grossman, Ron, and Charles Leroux. 1996. "A Local Outpost of Democracy." *Chicago Tribune,* March 5.

Guest, Avery, and Barrett Lee. 1983. "Consensus on Locality Names within the Metropolis." *Sociology and Social Research* 67: 374–91.

Gullestad, Marianne. 1984. *Kitchen Table Society.* Oslo, Norway: Hallestrom.

Guterbock, Thomas. 1980. *Machine Politics in Transition.* Chicago: University of Chicago Press.

Hadden, J., and J. Barton. 1979. "An Image That Will Not Die: Thoughts on the History of Anti-Urban Ideology." In *New Towns and the Suburban Dream,* edited by I. Allen. Port Washington, N.Y.: W. W. Norton.

Halle, David. 1984. *America's Working Man.* Chicago: University of Chicago Press.

———. 1990. "The Audience for Abstract Art." In *Cultivating Differences,* edited by Michèle Lamont and Marcel Fournier. Chicago: University of Chicago Press.

———. 1993. *Inside Culture.* Chicago: University of Chicago Press.

Hannerz, Ulf. 1969. *Soulside.* New York: Columbia University Press.

———. 1980. *Exploring the City.* New York: Columbia University Press.

Hartigan, John. 1999. *Racial Situations.* Princeton: Princeton University Press.

Hartman, C., et al. 1982. *Displacement: How to Fight It.* Berkeley, Calif.: National Housing Project.

Harvey, David. 1976. "Labor, Capital, and Class Struggle." *Politics and Society* 11: 265–95.

———. 1989a. *The Condition of Postmodernity* Cambridge, Mass: Blackwell.

———. 1989b. *The Urban Experience.* Baltimore: Johns Hopkins University Press.

Hawley, Amos. 1950. *Human Ecology.* New York: Ronald Press.

Hayden, D. 1984. *Redesigning the American Dream: The Future of Housing, Work, and Family Life.* New York: W. W. Norton.

Hedbige, Dick. 1979. *Subculture and the Meaning of Style.* New York: Methuen.

Hempel, D. J., and L. R. Tucker. 1979. "Citizen Preference for Housing as Common Social Indicators." *Environment and Behavior* 12: 399–428.

Heskin, A. 1981. "The History of Tenants in the U.S.: Struggle and Ideology." *International Journal of Urban and Regional Research* 5: 178–203.

Hirsch, Arnold. 1983. *Making the Second Ghetto.* Cambridge: Cambridge University Press.

Hochschild, Arlie. 1989. *The Second Shift.* New York: Avon.

Hummon, David. 1981. "House, Home, and Identity." In *Housing, Culture, and Design,* edited by Setha Low and Erve Chambers. Philadelphia: University of Pennsylvania Press.

————. 1985. "Urban Ideology as a Cultural System." *Journal of Cultural Geography* 5: 1–16.

————. 1990. *Commonplaces.* Albany: SUNY Press.

Hunter, Albert. 1978a. "Persistence of Local Sentiments in Mass Society." In *Handbook of Contemporary Urban Life,* edited by David Street et al. San Francisco: Jossey-Bass.

————. 1978b. *Symbolic Communities.* Chicago: University of Chicago Press.

Jackson, John B. 1994. *A Sense of Place, A Sense of Time.* New Haven: Yale University Press.

Jackson, Kenneth. 1985. *Crabgrass Frontier.* Oxford: Oxford University Press.

Jacobs, Jane. 1961. *The Death and Life of Great American Cities.* New York: Random House.

Janowitz, Morris. 1967. *The Community Press in an Urban Setting.* Chicago: University of Chicago.

Janowitz, Morris, and Gerald Suttles. 1977. "The Social Ecology of Citizenship." In *On Social Organization and Social Control,* edited by James Burk. Chicago: University of Chicago Press.

Kantowicz, Edward. 1975. *Polish-American Politics in Chicago.* Chicago: University of Chicago Press.

Karp, David, Gregory Stone, and William Yoels. 1977. *Being Urban.* Lexington, Mass.: D.C. Heath.

Kasarda, John, and Morris Janowitz. 1974. "Community Attachment in Mass Society." *American Sociological Review* 39: 28–39.

Katznelson, Ira. 1981. *City Trenches.* Chicago: University of Chicago Press.

Keith, Michael, and Steven Pile. 1988. *Place and the Politics of Identity.* London: Routledge.

Keller, Suzanne. 1968. *The Urban Neighborhood: A Sociological Perspective.* New York: Random House.

Kelling, George, and Catherine Coles. 1996. *Fixing Broken Windows.* New York: Touchstone.

Kohn, Melvin. 1977. *Class and Conformity.* Chicago: University of Chicago Press.

Komorovsky, Mirra. 1967. *Blue-Collar Marriage.* New York: Vintage Books.

Kornblum, William. 1974. *Blue Collar Community.* Chicago: University of Chicago Press.

Krase, Jerome. 1976. "Stigmatized Places, Stigmatized People: Crown Heights and Prospect-Lefferts." In *Brooklyn USA: The Fourth Largest City in America,* edited by Rita Seiden Miller. New York: Brooklyn College Press.

Kristol, Irving. 1995. "About Equality." In Kristol, *Neo-Conservatism: Selected Essays, 1949–1995.* New York: Free Press.

Lamarche, François. 1976. "Property Development and the Economic Foundations of the Urban Question." In *Urban Sociology: Critical Essays,* edited by C. G. Pickvance. New York: St. Martin's Press.

Lamont, Michèle. 1992. *Money, Morals, and Manners.* Chicago: University of Chicago Press.

———. 2000. *The Dignity of Working Men.* New York: Russell Sage and Cambridge: Harvard University Press.

Lamphere, Louise. 1977. *Working Daughters to Working Mothers.* Ithaca: Cornell University Press.

———. 1985. "Bringing the Family to Work: Women's Culture on the Shop Floor." *Feminist Studies* 11, no. 3: 519–40.

Lasch, Christopher. 1991. *The True and Only Heaven.* New York: W. W. Norton.

Laumann, Edward, and James House. 1970. "Living Room Styles and Social Attributes." In *Logic of Social Hierarchies,* edited by Edward Laumann, Paul Siegel, and Robert Hodge. Chicago: Markham.

Legett, John. 1968. *Working-Class Consciousness in Detroit.* New York: Oxford University Press.

Lemann, Nicholas. 1991. *The Promised Land.* New York: Knopf.

LeMasters, E. E. 1975. *Blue-Collar Aristocrats.* Madison: University of Wisconsin Press.

Levine, Adeline Gordon. 1982. *Love Canal: Science, Politics, and People.* Lexington, Mass.: D. C. Heath.

Levy, Frank. 1998. *The New Dollars and Dreams.* New York: Russell Sage Foundation.

Lewis, Oscar. 1951. *Life in the Mexican Village.* Urbana: University of Illinois Press.

———. 1965. "Further Observations on the Folk-Urban Continuum and Urbanization with Special Reference to Mexico City." In *The Study of Urbanization,* edited by Phillip Hauser and Leo Schnore. New York: Wiley.

———. 1966. *La Vida.* New York: Random House.

Liebow, Elliot. 1967. *Tally's Corner.* Boston: Little, Brown.

Lipinski, William. 1995. "Congressman Fears Loss of America's Middle Class." *Southwest News Herald* (Chicago),editorial, May 14.

Lofland, Lyn. 1973. *A World of Strangers.* New York: Basic Books.

Logan, John, and Harvey Molotch. 1987. *Urban Fortunes.* Berkeley and Los Angeles: University of California Press.

Lopata, Helena. 1971. *Occupation: Housewife.* New York: Oxford University Press.

Loyd, Bonnie. 1982. "Women, Home, and Status." In *Housing and Identity,* edited by James Duncan. New York: Holmes and Meier.

Lukas, J. Anthony. 1986. *Common Ground.* New York: Vintage Books.

Lynch, Kevin. 1960. *The Image of the City.* Cambridge: MIT Press.

Lynd, Robert S., and Helen Merrell Lynd. 1929. *Middletown.* New York: Harcourt Brace and Co.

Marcus, Steven. 1975. *Engels, Manchester, and the Working Class.* New York: Vintage Books.

Martindale, Don, and R. Galen Hanson. 1969. *Small Town and the Nation.* Westport, Conn.: Greenwood.

Marx, Leo. 1964. *The Machine in the Garden.* London: Oxford University Press.
———. 1984. "The Puzzle of Antiurbanism in Classic American Literature." In *Cities of the Mind,* edited by Lloyd Rodwin and Robert Hollister. New York: Plenum Press.

Massey, Doreen. 1994. *Space, Place, and Gender.* Minneapolis: University of Minnesota Press.

Massey, Doreen, and Pat Jess. 1995. *A Place in the World.* Oxford: Oxford University Press.

Massey, Douglas, and Nancy Denton. 1993. *American Apartheid.* Cambridge: Harvard University Press.

McGreevey, John. 1996. *Parish Boundaries.* Chicago: University of Chicago Press.

McMahon, Martha. 1995. *Engendering Motherhood.* New York: Guilford Press.

Meinig, Donald. 1979. "Symbolic Landscapes: Some Idealizations of American Communities." In *The Interpretation of Ordinary Landscapes: Geographical Essays,* edited by Donald Meinig. Oxford : Oxford University Press.

Miller, F. D., S. Tsemberis, G. P. Malia, and D. Grega. 1980. "Neighborhood Satisfaction among Urban Dwellers." *Journal of Social Issues* 36: 101–17.

Mollenkopf, John, and Manuel Castells. 1992. *Dual City.* New York: Russell Sage Foundation.

Molotch, Harvey. 1970. "Oil in Santa Barbara and Power in America." *Sociological Inquiry* 40: 131–44.

———. 1979. "Capital and Neighborhood in the United States." *Urban Affairs Quarterly* 14: 289–312.

Morely, David, and Kevin Robins. 1994. *Spaces of Identity.* New York: Routledge.

Morenoff, Jeffrey, and Robert Sampson. 1997. "Violent Crime and the Spatial Dynamics of Neighborhood Transition: Chicago, 1970–1990." *Social Forces* 76, no. 1: 31–64.

Newman, Katherine. 1988. *Falling from Grace.* New York: Vintage Books.

Nisbet, R. A. 1969. *The Quest for Community.* New York: Oxford University Press.

Oakley, Anne. 1974. *Housewife.* London: Allen Lane.

Packard, Vance. 1972. *A Nation of Strangers.* New York: McKay.

Park, Robert. 1925. "The City: Suggestions for the Investigation of Human Behavior." In *The City,* edited by Robert Park et al. Chicago: University of Chicago Press.

Patillo-McCoy, Mary. 1999. *Black Picket Fences.* Chicago: University of Chicago Press.

Peet, Richard. 1975. "Inequality and Poverty: A Marxist-Geographic Inquiry." *Annals of the Association of American Geographers,* 564–71.

Perin, Constance. 1977. *Everything in Its Place.* Princeton: Princeton University Press.

———. 1988. *Belonging in America.* Madison: University of Wisconsin Press.

Peshkin, Alan. 1978. *Growing Up American.* Chicago: University of Chicago Press.

Phillips, Susan A. 1999. *Wallbanging': Gangs and Grafitti in LA.* Chicago: University of Chicago Press.

Pickvance, C. G. 1984. "Spatial Policy as Territorial Politics." *Political Action and Social Identity,* edited by G. Rees. London: Macmillan.

Pritchett,. Wendell E. 2002. *Brownsville, Brooklyn: Blacks, Jews, and the Changing Face of the Ghetto.* Chicago: University of Chicago Press.

Protash, A., and M. Baldassare. 1983. "Growth Policies and Community Status." *Urban Affairs Quarterly* 18: 397–412.

Putnam, Robert. 1995. "Bowling Alone: America's Declining Social Capital." *Journal of Democracy* 6: 65–78.

Rainwater, Lee, Richard Coleman, and Gerald Handel. 1959. *Workingman's Wife*. New York: Oceana.

Rapoport, Amos. 1982. "Identity and Environment." In *Housing and Identity*, edited by James Duncan. New York: Holmes and Meier.

Relph, Edward. 1976. *Place and Placelessness*. London: Pion.

Rieder, Jonathan. 1985. *Canarsie*. Cambridge: Harvard University Press.

Riesman, David. 1958. "The Suburban Sadness." In *The Suburban Community*, edited by William Dobriner. New York: Putnam.

Rivlin, Leanne. 1982. "Group Membership and Place Meanings in an Urban Neighborhood." *Journal of Social Issues* 35: 75–93.

Rose, Gillian. 1993. *Feminism and Geography*. Cambridge, U.K.: Polity Press.

———. 1995. "Place and Identity: A Sense of Place." In *A Place in the World*, edited by Doreen Massey and Pat Jess. Oxford: Open University:

Rose, Tricia. 1994. *Black Noise*. Middletown, Conn.: University Press of New England.

Rourke, Francis E. 1964. "Urbanism and American Democracy." *Ethics* 74: 255–68.

Rowles, G. D. 1983. "Place and Personal Identity: Observations from Appalachia." *Journal of Environmental Psychology* 3: 299–313.

Rowles, Graham. 1980. *Prisoners of Space? Exploring the Geographical Experiences of Older People*. Boulder, Colo.: Westview Press.

Rubin, Lillian. 1972. *Busing and Backlash*. Berkeley and Los Angeles: University of California Press.

———. 1974. *Worlds of Pain*. New York: Harper.

———. 1994. *Families on the Fault Line*. New York: Basic Books.

Rutherford, John. 1990. "A Place Called Home: Identity and the Cultural Politics of Difference." In *Identity: Community, Culture, Difference*, edited by John Rutherford. London: Lawrence and Wishart.

Saegert, S. 1980. "Masculine Cities and Feminine Suburbs: Polarized Ideas, Contradictory Realities." *Signs* 2: 96–111.

Saegert, S., and G. Winkel. 1980. "The Home: A Critical Problem for Changing Sex Roles." In *New Space for Women*, edited by G. Wekerle, R. Patterson, and D. Morley. Boulder, Colo.: Westview Press.

Sampson, Robert J., Stephen W. Raudenbush, and Felton Earls. 1997. "Neighborhoods and Violent Crime: A Multilevel Study of Collective Efficacy." *Science* 277: 918–24.

Sears, David, and Jack Citrin. 1982. *Tax Revolt.* Cambridge: Harvard University Press.

Sennett, Richard. 1970. *The Uses of Disorder.* New York: Vintage Books.

Shields, Rob. 1991. *Places on the Margin.* London: Routledge.

Shostak, Arthur. 1969. *Blue-Collar Life.* Englewood Cliffs, N.J.: Prentice-Hall.

Shostak, Arthur, and William Gamburg. 1964. *Blue-Collar World.* Englewood Cliffs, N.J.: Prentice-Hall.

Simmel, Georg. 1971. "The Metropolis and Mental Life." In *Metropolis,* edited by Philip Kasinitz. New York: NYU Press:

Sinclair, Upton. 1906. *The Jungle.* New York: Penguin Books.

Skogan, Wesley. 1990. *Disorder and Decline.* New York: Free Press.

Snow, David, and Leon Anderson. 1993. *Down on Their Luck: A Study of Homeless Street People.* Berkeley and Los Angeles: University of California Press.

Spillman, Lyn. 1997. *Nation and Commemoration.* Cambridge: Cambridge University Press.

Stacey, Judith. 1990. *Brave New Families.* New York: Basic Books.

Stack, Carol. 1974. *All Our Kin.* New York: Harper and Row.

Steedman, Carolyn Kay. 1994. *Landscape for a Good Woman.* New Brunswick: Rutgers University Press.

Steinitz, Victoria, and Ellen Solomon. 1986. *Starting Out: Class and Community in the Lives of Working-Class Youth.* Philadelphia: Temple University Press.

Stinchcombe, Arthur. 1965. "Social Structure and Organizations." In *Handbook of Organizations,* edited by James March. New York: Rand McNally.

Strauss, Anselm. 1961. *Images of the American City.* New York: Free Press.

Sugrue, Thomas. 1996. *The Making of the Urban Crisis,* Princeton: Princeton University Press.

Sullivan, Mercer. 1989. *Getting Paid.* Ithaca: Cornell University Press.

Susman, Warren. 1985. *Culture as History.* New York: Pantheon Books.

Suttles, Gerald. 1968. *The Social Order of the Slum.* Chicago: University of Chicago Press.

———. 1972. *The Social Construction of Communities.* Chicago: University of Chicago Press.

―――. 1984. "The Cumulative Texture of Local Urban Culture." *American Journal of Sociology* 90: 83–302.

Taub, Richard P., D. Garth Taylor, and Jan D. Dunham. 1984. *Paths of Neighborhood Change.* Chicago: University of Chicago Press.

Tuan, Yi-Fu. 1974. *Topophilia.* Englewood Cliffs, N.J.: Prentice-Hall.

―――. 1977. *Space and Place: The Perspective of Experience.* Minneapolis: University of Minnesota Press.

―――. 1980. "Rootedness vs. Sense of Place." *Landscape* 1: 23–29.

Uchitelle, Louis. 2000. "Working Families Strain to Live Middle-Class Life." *New York Times,* September 10.

Urry, John. 1995. *Consuming Places.* London: Routledge.

Vanek, Joann. 1974. "Time Spent in Housework." *Scientific American* 231: 116–20.

Venkatesh, Sudhir. 2000. *American Project.* Cambridge: Harvard University Press.

Vidich, Arthur, and Joseph Bensman. 1960. *Small Town in Mass Society.* Princeton: Princeton University Press.

Warner, Sam. 1962. *Street Car Suburbs.* Cambridge: Harvard University Press.

Weber, Max. 1958. *The City.* New York: Free Press.

Wellman, Barry. 1979. "The Community Question: The Intimate Networks of East New Yorkers." *American Journal of Sociology* 84: 1201–31.

White, Morton, and Lucia White. 1964. *The Intellectual versus the City: From Thomas Jefferson to Frank Lloyd Wright.* New York: New American Library.

Whyte, William F. 1943. *Street Corner Society.* Chicago: University of Chicago Press.

Williams, Raymond. 1973. *The Country and the City.* New York: Oxford University Press.

Willis, Paul. 1977; 1981. *Learning to Labor.* New York: Columbia University Press.

―――. 1990. *Common Culture.* Boulder, Colo.: Westview Press.

Wilson, William J. 1978. *The Declining Significance of Race.* Chicago: University of Chicago Press.

―――. 1987. *The Truly Disadvantaged.* Chicago: University of Chicago Press.

Wirth, Louis. 1951[1938] "Urbanism as a Way of Life." *Cities and Societies,* edited by P. K. Hatt and A. J. Reiss. New York: Free Press.

Wolfe, Alan. 1998. *One Nation, After All.* New York: Viking Press.

Wright, Gwendolyn. 1980. *Moralism and the Model Home*. Chicago: University of Chicago Press.

Young, Iris. 1990. "The Ideal of Community." In *Feminism and Postmodernism,* edited by L. Nicholson. London: Routledge.

Young, Michael, and Peter Wilmott. 1992 [1957]. *Family and Kinship in East London*. Berkeley and Los Angeles: University of California Press.

Zorbaugh, Harvey. 1929. *The Gold Coast and the Slum*. Chicago: University of Chicago Press.

Zukin, Sharon. 1982. *Loft Living*. Baltimore: Johns Hopkins University Press.

———. 1993. *Landscapes of Power*. Berkeley and Los Angeles: University of California Press.

———. 1995. *The Cultures of Cities*. Cambridge, Mass.: Blackwell.

INDEX

Note: All locations are in Chicago unless otherwise noted. Chicago is noted where necessary to remove ambiguity.

Compositor: Impressions Book and Journal Services, Inc.
Text: 11/15 Granjon
Display: Granjon